HANDS-ON LEARNING!

More Than 1000 Activities for Young Children Using Everyday Objects

Gwen Snyder Kaltman

CORWIN

A SAGE Company

Disclaimer

Corwin and the author cannot be held responsible for damage, injury, or mishap incurred during the use of or because of any of the activities suggested in or by this book. The author recommends appropriate and reasonable caution and adult supervision of children based on the age and capability of each child. Children should not be left unattended at any time, and safety should be observed at all times.

For information:

Corwin
A SAGE Company
2455 Teller Road
Thousand Oaks, California 91320
(800) 233-9936
Fax: (800) 417-2466
www.corwinpress.com

SAGE Ltd.
1 Oliver's Yard
55 City Road
London EC1Y 1SP
United Kingdom

SAGE India Pvt. Ltd.
B 1/I 1 Mohan Cooperative
    Industrial Area
Mathura Road, New Delhi 110 044
India

SAGE Asia-Pacific Pte. Ltd.
33 Pekin Street #02-01
Far East Square
Singapore 048763

Printed in the United States of America.

Library of Congress Cataloging-in-Publication Data

Kaltman, Gwen Snyder.
Hands-on learning! : more than 1,000 activities for young children using everyday objects/Gwen Snyder Kaltman.
     p. cm.
Includes bibliographical references.
ISBN 978-1-4129-7094-5 (cloth)
ISBN 978-1-4129-7095-2 (pbk.)
    1. Early childhood education—Activity programs. I. Title.

LB1139.35.A37K35 2009
372.21—dc22   2008055973

This book is printed on acid-free paper.

09   10   11   12   13   10   9   8   7   6   5   4   3   2   1

Acquisitions Editor:	Jessica Allan
Editorial Assistant:	Joanna Coelho
Production Editor:	Eric Garner
Copy Editor:	Alison Hope
Typesetter:	C&M Digitals (P) Ltd.
Proofreader:	Charlotte Waisner
Cover Designer:	Rose Storey
Graphic Designer:	Karine Hovsepian

Contents

To Al—who is my critic, my advocate, my friend, my partner, my love

Acknowledgments

I owe a great debt to all the instructors, educational trainers, supervisors, directors, teachers, children, and families who have worked with me during my career. They influenced not just my work, but my life.

I want to thank my friend Judi Farber who read an early draft of the manuscript. She gave me honest feedback and ideas on everything from the content to the title of this book. I greatly appreciate both her friendship and wisdom. I also want to thank my husband, Al, and my sons, Mylan and Blaine, for their constant support, understanding, and suggestions.

This is the third book I have published with Corwin. They are a very professional organization with bright, caring people. I feel especially lucky to have worked with Jessica Allan, my editor. From the very first phone call when I explained my project, she was enthusiastic and supportive. I also want to thank my production editor, Eric Garner, and my copy editor, Alison Hope, for their help, patience, and understanding.

Additionally, Corwin gratefully acknowledges the following peer reviewers for their editorial insight and guidance:

Roxie R. Ahlbrecht
Second-Grade Classroom Teacher/Math Teacher Leader
Robert Frost Elementary
Sioux Falls, SD

Michelle Barnea
Early Childhood Consultant
Independent Consulting
Millburn, NJ

Susan E. Schipper
First-Grade Teacher
Charles Street Elementary School
Palmyra, NJ

About the Author

 **Gwen Snyder Kaltman** has spent more than 25 years working with young children, their families, and teachers. She is the author of *Help! For Teachers of Young Children: 88 Tips to Develop Children's Social Skills and Create Positive Teacher/Family Relationships* and *More Help! For Teachers of Young Children: 99 Tips to Promote Intellectual Development and Creativity*. Kaltman earned her B.S. and M.Ed. in Early Childhood Education from the University of Maryland, and has been a preschool teacher, director, college instructor, and educational trainer in various parts of the country. She has also been a validator for the National Academy of Early Childhood Programs, which is the accreditation division of the National Association for the Education of Young Children.

Kaltman has worked with young children in Connecticut, Delaware, Georgia, Maryland, Massachusetts, New York, Tennessee, and Virginia. She has trained teachers working in Head Start programs in Chattanooga, Tennessee, and rural Georgia, and in daycare centers and preschools in the suburbs of New York City and Washington, DC. Kaltman has observed preschool classes in such diverse places as China, Easter Island, Greenland, India, Malta, Mongolia, Tibet, Tanzania, Venezuela, and native villages above the Arctic Circle and along the Amazon and Sepik rivers.

Born and raised in the Bedford-Stuyvesant section of Brooklyn, New York, she has been married for over 30 years. While it is true that her gray hairs started growing when she was in high school, she attributes most of them to her two sons.

If you have ideas or suggestions that you would like to share, Gwen would love to hear from you. Please email them to her at gwenkaltman@hotmail.com. Be sure to include your name so she can acknowledge you if your material is included in a future publication. Thank you for sharing!

Introduction

"What should we do next week?" is a question that teachers of young children wrestle with all year long. Good teachers are always looking for new ideas and activities. This is a book of hands-on themes and activities that you will want to try out in your classroom. More importantly, this book shows you a new way to design lesson plans—one that will guarantee hands-on experiential learning opportunities for young children.

The themes in this book are based on what is in the child's immediate environment, the here-and-now world of the young child. All the objects and materials needed are found close at hand. They are things that the children are likely to encounter at home, in their neighborhood, or at school. When you use objects and materials that young children are familiar with, you can build on and expand the children's knowledge as well as connect the children's experiences to classroom activities.

This book should be used to enrich your current program. It is arranged so that it can be used in at least five different ways:

1. You can use it to take advantage of child-initiated activities. For example, when a child comes to school delighted with new shoes or ribbons in her hair, you can use the themes and activities in this book to expand and develop the children's interest in that topic.

2. You can choose to do a particular theme, and select some or all of the hands-on activities developed specifically for that theme.

3. You can select hands-on activities that focus on literacy, mathematics, science, social studies, physical development, or creativity without relating them to a specific theme.

4. You can pick and choose (cherry pick) hands-on activities to broaden and enrich your curriculum.

5. You can use the new way to design themes and activities introduced in this book to create your own hands-on themes and activities. A list of suggestions for developing tactile activities is included as a resource to help you develop hands-on activities in literacy, mathematics, science, social studies, physical development, and creativity.

I begin each theme with a brief introduction and then list some facts or concepts that the children may discover as a result of doing the activities. For ease of communication, the activities for each of the themes in this book are grouped into sections on literacy, mathematics, science, social studies, physical development, and creativity. However, keep in mind that learning cannot be compartmentalized. For example, making muffins involves literacy (reading a recipe), mathematics (measuring ingredients), social studies (cooperating with classmates), science (observing the effects of heat on the batter), physical development (pouring and stirring the ingredients), and creativity (decorating the muffins).

Many of the activities in this book can be done with individuals or small groups of children. To help you be more responsive to the developmental needs of individual children, I make suggestions throughout the book on how to modify activities to make them simpler or more challenging. View every activity as an opportunity to help each child develop a positive self-image and master the art of getting along with others. When selecting activities, be sensitive to the beliefs and customs of children from different cultural and religious backgrounds. Whatever activities you choose, be sure the children enjoy what they are doing and do not become frustrated. Remember that children are always learning, and the most important thing we can teach children is the love of learning.

Part I

How to Create Hands-On Learning Opportunities

1

A New Way to Design Themes and Activities for Young Children

Wisdom is the daughter of experience.

—Leonardo da Vinci

This book provides activities that you will want to try out in your classroom. It also presents a new way to design themes and activities, one that will guarantee hands-on experiential learning opportunities for young children.

Whether you are reviewing work by Froebel, Piaget, Vygotsky, or the Constructivists, psychologists and educators agree that a developmentally appropriate curriculum for young children needs to emphasize the children's interactions with their immediate environment. This view also is supported by recent neuroscience and brain-based research, which emphasizes that children need hands-on experiential learning opportunities.

The National Association for the Education of Young Children's (NAEYC's) position statement on developmentally appropriate practices notes that "children are active learners, drawing on direct physical and social experience" and that developmentally appropriate practices must "include children's exposure to physical knowledge, learned through firsthand experience of using objects." The High/Scope Educational Research Foundation's active participatory learning curriculum is based on the principle that "children and adults learn best through hands-on experiences with people, materials, events, and ideas," and The Creative Curriculum is grounded in child development theory and research that stresses the importance of hands-on learning.

Young children learn through their five senses, so teachers should provide experiences that allow children to touch, see, smell, taste, and hear. Developmentally appropriate lesson plans reflect the fact that children learn through play and activity. Children need hands-on experiences that enable them to observe and manipulate objects and materials. When designing lesson plans, teachers should focus on what the children will be doing, and on what objects and materials they can provide for the children to handle and observe.

Trying to select themes and develop activities that are developmentally appropriate can be a challenge. One popular approach is for teachers to first decide on a theme, and then gather materials and plan activities to support that theme. I suggest you try a new way to select some of your themes, one that will help you provide additional hands-on learning experiences for young children. Instead of choosing a general theme and then developing activities to support that theme, first think about an object or material that the children can observe, handle, and interact with. Then, develop activities using that object or material. This new approach requires a paradigm shift; it is hands-on learning taken to the extreme.

This book demonstrates how to choose objects and materials and then build developmentally appropriate themes and activities that by their very nature will guarantee hands-on learning experiences. This new approach of creating tactile (object- or material-based) themes should be used to enrich and expand your current program, not replace it. Tactile themes can be used to supplement any curriculum. Whether you use High/Scope, The Creative Curriculum, an emergent curriculum, or incorporate NAEYC developmentally appropriate practices into your own curriculum, this new way of selecting themes and developing activities by focusing on objects and materials will help you provide hands-on learning experiences.

To help you explain tactile themes to parents and families, I have included a sample letter to them in the appendix. This letter discusses the importance of hands-on learning and the use of tactile themes. Feel free to modify the letter to suit your particular situation.

The tactile themes and activities in this book are just a sample of what you can do. My purpose is to inspire by example and to help you become comfortable with the approach of selecting objects and materials first and then building themes and activities around them. Using this new approach, I am certain that when you look around your classroom, home, and neighborhood you will be able to find many objects and materials that you can use to design developmentally appropriate themes to enrich and expand your program, and guarantee hands-on learning experiences for the children in your care.

Once you are familiar with the tactile themes and activities in this book, you should be ready to use this new approach of first choosing objects and materials and then building themes and activities around them. To help you get started I have included

> suggestions for developing hands-on activities in literacy, mathematics, science, social studies, physical development, and creativity; and

> activities for the theme boxes. For these activities, I have indicated some of the specific learning that can occur with each activity.

Before deciding to use an object or material, think about the following:

1. Safety. Is the object or material age appropriate for the children to handle and work with? Will the object or material break or tear easily, or will activities using the object or material require close adult supervision?

2. Size. Is the object or material too large or too small for the children to manage on their own?

3. Appeal. Will the children readily work with the object or material?

4. Availability. Can you provide generous amounts of the object or material for the children to interact with?

5. Attitude. Most important of all is your attitude. Will you convey a positive attitude toward the children as they handle and interact with the object or material?

When you are developing lesson plans, think creatively. Themes can be merged or contrasted, and there is no rule concerning appropriate time limits when it comes to doing a theme. Unfortunately, some teachers think about lesson plans in terms of a five-day block of time: Monday through Friday. Children need time to reflect and make comparisons. There is no reason why the children cannot study a subject for two weeks or two months. Be flexible. What should determine the time spent on a theme is the children's interest level. Observe the children carefully. Their questions, responses, and actions should help guide you to new themes and activities.

You may find it easier to develop activities for some objects or materials than for others. If you are unable to develop several hands-on activities for a theme, it is a warning sign that the theme may not be developmentally appropriate for the children in your care. Do not be discouraged if your initial attempts do not work out as well as you had hoped. Give yourself time to adjust to this new approach to selecting themes and developing activities.

Remember that the tactile themes in this book and the additional themes that you choose to develop using this new approach should be used to enrich your current program, not replace it. When you are ready to develop your own tactile themes and activities, use the following overview as a guide, keeping in mind that learning cannot be compartmentalized.

Literacy is more than learning the ABCs. It involves all aspects of language. Reading is about the meaning of words. To comprehend the written word children must have many experiences so they can relate to the ideas being presented in a book. Literacy activities include but are not limited to

- opportunities to talk (express ideas) and listen,
- vocabulary development,
- visual discrimination,
- letter recognition—upper and lowercase,
- phonological awareness,
- reading experiences,
- writing experiences, and
- dramatic play.

Mathematics is not just about numbers. Mathematical activities should involve logical thinking and include but not be limited to

- mathematical vocabulary,
- rote counting,
- one-to-one correspondence,
- number recognition,
- fractions,
- seriating and ordering,
- estimating,
- measuring,
- weighing,
- pattern recognition,
- creating and reading graphs,
- geometric figures and shapes, and
- spatial relationships.

Science for the young child is about using the five senses, observing, and wondering. Set up experiments with the children's help and invite the children to speculate about what might happen. Do not concern yourself if some experiments do not work out as planned. It is the process and not the outcome that is important. Scientific activities include but are not limited to

- scientific vocabulary,
- using the five senses,
- speculating and wondering,
- experimenting,
- developing observation skills,
- making comparisons,
- studying cause and effect,
- sequencing,

- using scientific equipment,
- classifying (using both child- and adult-suggested criteria), and
- observing and caring for people, plants, and animals.

Social studies for the young child begins with developing a positive self image. When children feel good about themselves, it is easier for them to relate positively to others and function as an individual that is part of a community. We need to provide experiences that help children learn to value themselves, their families, and other individuals, including those from different cultural, ethnic, racial, and religious backgrounds. We also need to provide opportunities to avoid stereotyping and sexism by emphasizing the sameness of different peoples and their positive contributions to the community. Social studies helps children understand and develop a connection to the larger community that includes their school and neighborhood. Social studies activities include but are not limited to

- learning about yourself and your family,
- learning about other children and their families,
- learning about different cultures,
- valuing different peoples and their customs,
- learning to avoid sexism and stereotyping,
- learning how to cooperate with others,
- dramatic play,
- developing an understanding and connection to the community,
- trips and demonstrations,
- developing a responsible attitude toward the environment, and
- developing a sense of social and community responsibility.

Physical development is every bit as important as intellectual development. Physical development activities include but are not limited to

- gross motor control,
- fine motor control,
- eye-hand coordination,
- eye-foot coordination,
- spatial awareness,
- temporal awareness,
- sensory awareness,
- body awareness, and
- balance skills.

Creativity involves more than doing music and art activities. It is a way of approaching the world. We need to plan activities that will encourage divergent

(Continued)

(Continued)

thinking, adaptability, and flexibility of thought in young children. Activities to foster creativity should be a part of all aspects of the curriculum and include but not be limited to

- stimulating thoughts and ideas,
- fostering an attitude of acceptance toward trying new ideas,
- encouraging the children to think of and try multiple ways to solve a problem,
- using materials in new and different ways,
- open-ended art experiences,
- movement,
- music, and
- dramatic play.

2

Suggestions for Developing Hands-On Activities

Literacy, Mathematics, Science, Social Studies, Physical Development, and Creativity

After you have done a few of the themes in this book, you will notice that some of the activities seem familiar and have been used in a different form in more than one theme. Repetition is an important part of learning. For example, when we teach number concepts such as one-to-one correspondence, we ask the children to count different objects time and time again. I believe that a good activity not only can, but also *should* be used more than once. For example, when trying to familiarize children with letters, you can create three different activities by asking the children to match letters printed on index cards to letters printed on boxes, on bags, and on envelopes. When trying to help children learn about sequencing and patterns you can invite the children to match patterns using different materials—for example, ribbons, colored plastic spoons, and cotton balls.

To help you design original activities for your own themes, I have grouped activities that can be repeated multiple times using different objects or materials under the headings of literacy, mathematics, science, social studies, physical development, and creativity. The activities will seem new to the children each time because they are using different objects or materials. When developing your plans, try to think about the unique properties of the object or material that you are focusing on. Each object or material has its own characteristics; it is these characteristics that offer variety. For example, water can be frozen, balls can be rolled, and ribbons can be cut and bent. Use the following suggestions for developing tactile activities as a resource when you are trying to develop your own hands-on activities.

LITERACY

1. Provide opportunities for the children to sort or match the objects or materials by color.

2. Provide opportunities for the children to find or match letters using the objects or materials. For example, look for specific letters printed on a cereal box.

3. Invite the children to form letters using the objects or materials.

4. Invite the children to create signs, draw pictures, or dictate or write stories involving the object or material.

5. Provide opportunities for the children to increase their phonological awareness. For example, create activities where the children look for or identify items that either rhyme or begin with the same sound as the object or material.

6. Create a game where you ask the children to match the object or material to items that are associated with that object or material. For example, the children could match soupspoon to soup.

7. Create original puzzles that make use of the object or material. For example, cut a cereal box into several pieces.

8. Provide opportunities for the children to read (follow printed) recipes or instructions involving the object or material.

9. Invite the children to use the object or material to create or use with puppets.

10. Provide opportunities for dramatic play using the object or material.

11. Provide opportunities for discussion by inviting the children to bring examples of the object or material from their home.

12. Use open-ended questions to stimulate discussion about the object or material.

13. Read and discuss books that involve the object or material.

14. Organize treasure hunts or walks to collect the object or material.

15. Provide opportunities to develop vocabulary by discussing with the children words they could use to describe the objects or materials (adjectives), or how the objects or materials are alike or different.

MATHEMATICS

1. Provide opportunities for the children to count the objects or materials.

2. Provide opportunities for the children to measure the objects or materials.

3. Provide opportunities for the children to weigh the objects or materials.

4. Provide opportunities for the children to order the objects or materials by size or weight.

5. Use the object or material to provide opportunities for the children to talk about temperature or time.

6. Invite the children to create graphs about the objects or materials.

7. Create original games involving the objects or materials that use a die or spinners to encourage counting or number recognition.

8. Create pattern sequences using the objects or materials and ask the children to match your pattern.

9. Provide opportunities for the children to estimate. For example, ask the children to guess how many objects there are in a container.

10. Provide opportunities for the children to increase their awareness of spatial relationships; for example, guess how many objects such as shoes, ribbons, or toilet paper rolls will fit in a container.

11. Provide opportunities for the children to use the objects or materials to create or work with geometric shapes.

12. Provide opportunities for the children to become familiar with fractions by cutting the object or material in half, thirds, and quarters.

SCIENCE

1. Provide opportunities for the children to use the object or material to conduct or observe experiments and to study cause and effect; for example, "I wonder what will happen if . . . ."

2. Provide opportunities for the children to use the object or material to develop observation skills; for example, will it sink or float?

3. Provide opportunities for the children to use their sense of hearing and experiment with sound using the object or material.

4. Use the object or material to provide opportunities for the children to use their sense of touch.

5. Use the object or material to provide opportunities for the children to use their sense of smell.

6. Provide opportunities for the children to use their sense of taste. Use the object or material when preparing or consuming food.

7. Provide opportunities for the children to use the object or material to experiment with light and shadows.

8. Provide opportunities for the children to inspect the object or material with a magnifying glass.

9. Provide opportunities for the children to collect, compare, contrast, and classify the objects or materials.

10. Provide opportunities for the children to use the object or material with equipment such as magnets, levers, gears, and pulleys.

11. Provide opportunities for the children to observe physical changes in the object or material.

12. Provide opportunities for the children to observe the effects of gravity on the objects or materials.

13. Provide opportunities for the children to observe the effects of air, water, heat, and cold on the objects or materials.

SOCIAL STUDIES

1. Provide opportunities for the children to learn about themselves and one another by inviting family members to class to discuss holidays and traditions, and to share folk tales, stories, music, food, or dances that involve the object or material. If family members cannot come to class, encourage them to send in objects or materials that can be shared with the children.

2. Arrange a trip to visit someone's home or somewhere else to observe the object or material.

3. Invite guests (human, animal, vegetable, or mineral) into your classroom, and demonstrate the use of the object or material.

4. Organize a parade or a special social event involving the object or material. Invite another class, school staff, family members, or senior citizens to the event.

5. Make arrangements for the children to attend a sporting event or performance, or observe a rehearsal or team practice in which the object or material is used.

6. Provide opportunities for the children to learn simple games, songs, or dances from other cultures that involve the object or material.

7. Provide opportunities for the children to taste or prepare foods from different cultures using the object or material.

8. Provide opportunities for the children to hear different languages spoken. Play songs sung in other languages or invite someone in to read a short simple story about the object or material in another language. Translate for the children after each paragraph is read.

9. Provide opportunities for the children to enjoy examples of artwork from different cultures that feature or make use of the object or material.

10. Provide opportunities for the children to engage in cooperative activities or projects using the object or material.

11. Provide opportunities for the children to develop a sense of social and community responsibility by reaching out to others in the community using the

object or material. For example, the children could create works of art using the object or material and then give them to a senior citizens center.

12. Provide opportunities for the children to help take care of the environment using the object or material. For example, use boxes as part of a clean-up-the-yard day.

13. To help develop social skills and cooperation, provide opportunities for dramatic play using the object or material.

PHYSICAL DEVELOPMENT

1. Provide opportunities for the children to toss, catch, kick, roll, cut, bend, fold, twist, shred, thread, balance, or stack the objects or materials.

2. Create an obstacle course and provide opportunities for the children to jump over or go under, through, or to the left or right of the objects or materials.

3. Provide opportunities for the children to slide, crawl, roll, walk on tiptoes, and move forward, backward, up, down, or sideways with the objects or materials.

4. Provide opportunities for the children to move the objects or materials quickly or slowly.

5. Provide opportunities for the children to lift, carry, or push the objects or materials.

6. Provide opportunities for the children to kick and throw the objects or materials at targets.

CREATIVITY

1. Provide opportunities for the children to think about new ways to use the object or material.

2. Ask the children how they would modify the object or material, improve it, or make it larger or smaller.

3. Discuss different ways to solve a problem that involves the object or material. For example, ask the children how they would move a heavy box from one location to another.

4. Invite the children to decorate the object or use the material to decorate something.

5. Invite the children to design a game using the object or material.

6. Ask the children to suggest a way to do a movement activity with the object or material.

7. Ask the children to create a chant, song, or poem about the object or material.

8. Encourage dramatic play using the object or material.

9. Provide opportunities for the children to dance or move to music while using the object or material.

10. Provide opportunities for the children to make instruments using the object or material, and then use the instruments with or without musical accompaniment.

3

Boxes as a Theme

Highlighting Some of the Specific Learning That Can Occur With Each Activity

Boxes come in many sizes, shapes, and materials (for example, cardboard, wood, metal, and plastic). Collect as many different types of boxes as possible, everything from small jewelry boxes to large boxes for shipping a refrigerator or TV set. Try to include cereal, toothpaste, and plastic airtight food storage boxes. The more variety, the better. It will take some time to gather the boxes you will need. If storage space becomes an issue, some cardboard boxes can be opened and made flat until it is time to use them. When doing this theme or any other theme, encourage the children to think "outside the box."

HELP CHILDREN DISCOVER

1. Boxes are made of many different materials.

2. Boxes come in different sizes and shapes.

3. Boxes are used for different purposes.

4. Some boxes are specifically designed for special items, such as eggs or tissues.

LITERACY

1. Create a puzzle for the children by cutting the front or back panel of a cereal box (or any box with a simple colorful design) into several pieces. To make this activity more challenging, cut the panel into more pieces. (Visual discrimination)

2. Print a letter on an index card and then ask the children to find the same letter printed on a box. This activity can be made more challenging by asking the children to find an upper- or lowercase letter. For example, find A, b, or C, or find a particular letter without the aid of a letter printed on an index card. (Letter recognition)

3. Place a few boxes on the floor. Label each box with a different letter of the alphabet. On a table, have index cards printed with the same letters that appear on the boxes. Invite the children to toss a beanbag into a box. Then, ask the children to match the letter on the box that the beanbag landed in to a letter on the table. This activity can be made more challenging by using upper- and lowercase letters or simple words. It can be made simpler by using colors instead of letters or words. (Letter recognition)

4. Bring in boxes that are used for take-out food from restaurants, such as Chinese meals, pizza pies, or sandwiches. Encourage the children to examine the boxes and discuss what foods might come in the boxes, and what foods they like to eat. This activity presents a good opportunity to discuss nutrition. (Opportunities to talk and listen)

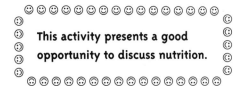

This activity presents a good opportunity to discuss nutrition.

5. Draw or paste a picture of an item, such as a hat, on a box. Discuss rhyming words with the children. Then, challenge the children to find things in the room that rhyme with that item and put them in the box. The children may find things such as a toy cat, a small bat, or a mat. You could also use a letter instead of a picture, and ask the children to find things that begin with the same sound as the letter. For example, if you print the letter M the children could find mittens, markers, money, or mail. (Phonological awareness)

6. Use small boxes without lids to create a concentration game. Print letters on small pieces of paper. Be sure to print each letter at least twice. I suggest starting with three or four different letters. Turn the boxes upside down and place one letter under each box. Challenge the children to lift the boxes and find the matching letters. This activity can be made more challenging by using more letters, upper- and lowercase letters or, if the children are ready, by using small words. (Letter recognition)

7. Invite the children to decorate a shoebox and use it as a mailbox. Encourage the children to send notes or drawings to one another. (Writing experiences, Reading experiences)

8. Put some boxes in the housekeeping corner and invite the children to pretend it is moving day, or to use the boxes anyway they like. (Dramatic play)

9. Color a small box (or just paste a piece of construction paper on the box), and then ask the children to find items to put in the box that match that color. Children can find crayons, markers, small blocks, or manipulatives that are the same color. To make this activity more challenging, instead of providing a sample of the color, print the color word on the box. (Visual discrimination, Reading experiences)

10. On the inside of a medium-size shirt or shoebox, trace patterns for some of the different tools that are kept in a toolbox, such as a hammer, small saw, and

screwdriver. Invite the children to find the tools that match the patterns. (Visual discrimination)

11. Create a prop box. Put a few items in a box and encourage the children to create a story that involves the props. (Opportunities to talk and listen)

12. Read the book *Whistle for Willie* by Ezra Jack Keats. Discuss with the children why Peter hides under a large cardboard box at the end of the story. Ask the children if the dog could have found the boy even if he had not whistled. (Reading experiences)

13. Stimulate language by creating a feely box. Cut a hole large enough for a child to put his hand into a medium-size box (such as a shoebox). Place an item in the box and then ask a child to reach in the box and describe or talk about what he feels. (Vocabulary development)

14. Cut a hole in a large box so that it resembles a TV set. Encourage the children to pretend they are on television. They could be announcers, singers, actors, or actresses. (Dramatic play)

15. Make garages out of shoeboxes or other small boxes. Cut a hole in the side of each box to represent a garage door. Identify each garage by writing a letter above or on the side of the door. Paste the same letters on small toy cars, and then ask the children to park each car in the garage with the matching letter. This activity can be made more challenging by using simple words rather than just letters. It can be made simpler by using colors instead of letters. (Visual discrimination, Letter recognition)

16. Place an assortment of boxes on a table for the children to handle and examine. Discuss with the children words that they could use to describe the different boxes, or how the boxes are alike and different. (Opportunities to talk and listen, Vocabulary development)

MATHEMATICS

1. Invite the children to fill a few small boxes of identical size with different items such as cotton, sand, or pebbles. Then, ask the children to weigh the boxes, or order the boxes from the lightest to the heaviest. To make this activity more challenging increase the number of boxes used. (Weighing, Seriating and ordering)

2. Place several different-size boxes and lids on a table. Challenge the children to find the lids that fit on each box. (Spatial relationships)

3. Provide the children with an assortment of boxes. Ask the children to order or sort them by size. Use words like small, medium, large, larger, largest, bigger, and biggest. (Seriating and ordering, Mathematical vocabulary)

4. Challenge the children to look for and count the number of boxes in the room. (One-to-one correspondence)

5. Invite the children to guess how many items, such as toy trucks or blocks, will fit in a box. Then, with the children, count how many of the items fit in the box. This activity can be made more challenging by increasing the size of the box (thereby increasing its capacity) or by using smaller items. For example, start with large toy trucks, and then use smaller toy cars. (Estimating, One-to-one correspondence, Spatial relationships)

6. Write a number in each compartment of an egg carton and invite the children to put that number of small items (for example, seeds) in each compartment. (Number recognition, One-to-one correspondence)

7. Create a geometric shape box by cutting circle, triangle, rectangle, and square openings on each side of the box. Ask the children to put cutout shapes that you have prepared in the appropriate openings. (Geometric figures and shapes, Spatial relationships)

8. Invite the children to measure paper and ribbon to gift-wrap a box. (Measuring)

9. Give a child a box that contains a piece of paper with a number written on it. Ask the child to find the number of items that match the number that is written on the piece of paper and will fit inside the box. To make this activity more challenging you can write increasingly higher numbers. This is a good spatial relationship activity because the children will need to choose smaller items to place in the box as the number of items increases. To make this activity even more challenging, ask the child to find specific items to put in the box, for example, items that are round, or round and green. (Number recognition, One-to-one correspondence, Spatial relationships, Geometric figures and shapes,)

> This is a good spatial relationship activity because the children will need to choose smaller items to place in the box as the number of items increases.

10. Create a game using a die. Give a child an empty tissue box. Ask the child to roll the die and then put the corresponding number of tokens into the box. The game is over when all the tokens have been used up. Some children may wish to count the number of tokens in their box. To make this game simpler, create a die with only one, two, and three dots. (One-to-one correspondence)

11. Invite the children to create a tower using boxes, and then count the boxes. (One-to-one correspondence)

12. Provide the children with an assortment of boxes. Ask the children to sort the boxes by shape. Cheese often comes in a circular shaped box, Toblerone chocolate comes in a triangular shaped box, and many items come in square and rectangular shaped boxes. (Geometric figures and shapes)

SCIENCE

1. Invite the children to listen for different sounds as they tap a box with different items. For example, have the children use a spoon, stick, or feather to tap a box. To

make this activity more challenging, ask the children to compare the sounds they make when they tap boxes of different sizes or boxes made of different materials such as cardboard and wood. (Using the five senses, Experimenting)

2. Place rubber bands over different-size openings on boxes made of different materials. Invite the children to listen to the sounds and feel the vibrations that are made when the rubber bands are plucked. (Using the five senses, Studying cause and effect)

3. Create a game. Glue samples of products to index cards and then ask the children to find the boxes the products come in. For example, tissues and tissue box, spaghetti and spaghetti box, and crayons and crayon box. (Classifying)

4. Place an assortment of plastic and metal boxes on a table near a window where sunbeams are shining into the room. Invite the children to use the different boxes to try to catch and reflect the sunlight onto a nearby wall. Let the children discover which boxes work best. (Developing observation skills, Making comparisons, Studying cause and effect)

5. Out of the sight of the other children, ask a child to talk into an empty box. Challenge the children to identify who is talking. You could also place several different-size boxes on a table and encourage the children to experiment with sound by making noises or talking into the empty boxes. (Using the five senses, Studying cause and effect)

6. Put water in the sensory table. With the children, place boxes made of different materials such as wood, cardboard, and plastic into the water. Be sure to include a few plastic airtight food boxes (such as Ziploc) that have their lids properly closed. Ask the children to speculate about what will happen to the boxes. Invite the children to examine the boxes after an hour or two. You could also encourage the children to speculate about which boxes will sink or float. (Speculating and wondering, Developing observation skills, Making comparisons, Studying cause and effect)

7. Place an assortment of boxes on a table and ask the children to sort the boxes by their purpose, such as boxes used for food, toys, or clothing. (Classifying)

8. Without the children observing, place different items such as sand, golf balls, rocks, spoons, and coins in small boxes and seal them. Invite the children to shake the boxes and listen carefully. Then, ask the children to identify the items in the boxes. This activity can be made simpler by placing samples of the items that are in the boxes on a table for the children to choose from. (Using the five senses)

9. Invite the children to figure out how the music starts and stops in a music box. (Speculating and wondering, Developing observation skills, Studying cause and effect)

10. Place an assortment of boxes made of different materials on a table or on the floor. Invite the children to use a magnifying glass to closely inspect the boxes. (Using scientific equipment, Developing observation skills)

11. Remove the lid from a shoebox. Place a few items in the shoebox, such as a crayon, a pair of metal scissors, and a jumbo-size metal paper clip. Invite the children to move a magnet along the outside bottom panel of the shoebox and observe what happens. Encourage the children to experiment and put other items in the shoebox. Then, do this same activity using magnets with different strengths and boxes made of other materials. (Using scientific equipment, Experimenting, Developing observation skills, Studying cause and effect)

SOCIAL STUDIES

1. Invite each child to create a treasure box. Ask each child to bring a few items from home to put in his box. Invite the children to talk about what is in their treasure boxes. (Learning about oneself, Learning about other children and their families, Valuing different people and their customs)

2. Invite to class a family member or someone else who enjoys fishing. Ask the person to show the children a tackle box, what is inside the box, and how it is used. (Learning about other children and their families, Trips and demonstrations)

3. Bring in boxes that have ingredients or instructions printed in different languages. Encourage the children to examine the different ways of writing. (Learning about different cultures, Valuing different people and their customs)

4. In the bottom of a shirt box, cut a few holes large enough for a small toy to fall through. Place a toy in the box, then invite one child to hold one end of the box and another child to hold the other end of the box. Challenge the children to cooperate and try to tilt the box to make the toy slide and fall through one of the holes. To make this activity more challenging, cut only one or two holes in the box. (Learning how to cooperate with others)

5. Visit a warehouse-type supermarket and observe all the different boxes. Try to arrange to see boxes opened and unpacked. (Developing an understanding and connection to the community)

6. Invite someone in to discuss Boxing Day, a holiday celebrated on December 26 in Great Britain, Australia, Canada, New Zealand, and a number of other nations. Traditionally, Boxing Day is when employers gave gifts (Christmas boxes) to their employees. (Learning about different cultures, Valuing different peoples and their customs)

7. Visit a large appliance store and observe big boxes. Try to arrange to see a truck being unloaded. (Trips and demonstrations)

8. Organize a project to cheer someone up. Ask the children to fill a small box with pictures, drawings, written notes, or things that they have made, then send the box to a person who is ill or to a senior citizens center. (Developing a sense of social and community responsibility)

9. Visit a jewelry store and observe small boxes. (Trips and demonstrations)

10. Visit a bank and see the safe deposit boxes. (Developing an understanding and connection to the community, Trips and demonstrations)

11. Invite the children to decorate a large box and create a puppet stage. Encourage the children to put on puppet shows for each other or for other classes. (Learning how to cooperate with others)

12. Try to observe a moving truck crew and watch how they lift heavy boxes, or arrange to see the delivery of some large boxes to your center. If possible, meet a female member of a moving crew or delivery person. (Learning to avoid sexism and stereotyping, Trips and demonstrations)

13. Invite to class a family member or someone else who collects music boxes. Ask the person to show some of the music boxes in her collection to the children. (Learning about other children and their families)

14. Organize a clean-up-the-yard day. Invite the children to collect trash and place it in cardboard boxes. (Developing a responsible attitude toward the environment)

PHYSICAL DEVELOPMENT

1. Fill a small- to medium-size box with sand or scraps of crumpled up paper. Hide a few tokens or small toys in the box under the sand or paper. Challenge the children to put a hand in the box and find the hidden treasures. (Fine motor control)

2. Draw a shape or simple picture on a panel from a cereal or gift box to create a lacing card. Punch holes on the outline of the shape and invite the children to use ribbon to lace through the holes. To make it easier for the children to thread the ribbon, create a pointed end by wrapping a piece of masking tape around one end of the ribbon. (Eye-hand coordination)

> To make it easier for the children to thread the ribbon, create a pointed end by wrapping a piece of masking tape around one end of the ribbon.

3. Ask the children to use tweezers to put small items such as crumpled pieces of tissue paper or cotton balls in a box. This activity can be made simpler by asking the children to pick up the items with their fingers. (Eye-hand coordination, Fine motor control)

4. Invite the children to use shoeboxes as pretend big shoes to walk in. (Gross motor control)

5. Provide a large box for the children to play Jack-in-the-Box. (Temporal awareness, Gross motor control)

6. Create an obstacle course where the children climb over, under, and through boxes of different sizes. (Spatial awareness, Gross motor control)

7. Challenge the children to balance a small box in the palm of one hand and walk from Point A to Point B. A variation on this activity would be to invite the children to carry a box while walking on a balance beam. (Balance skills, Body awareness)

8. Cut a hole in a large box and invite the children to use it for a beanbag toss game. To make this activity more challenging, cut a smaller hole or increase the distance the children have to toss the beanbag to reach the box. (Gross motor control)

9. Challenge the children to see how many boxes they can carry. (Gross motor control)

10. Invite the children to use keys to open locks on boxes. (Fine motor control, Eye-hand coordination)

11. Invite the children to kick boxes of different sizes from Point A to Point B. (Eye-foot coordination, Gross motor control)

CREATIVITY

1. Ask the children to pretend that there is a very heavy box in the room next door that needs to be moved to the office. Discuss with the children their ideas for moving the box. (Encouraging the children to think of and try multiple ways to solve a problem)

2. Invite the children to examine an open lunch box and discuss what they might put in it. (Using materials in new and different ways)

3. Place a large box in the classroom or on the playground where the children can pretend to be in an airplane, car, cave, or whatever they choose to imagine. (Fostering an attitude of acceptance toward trying new ideas, Using materials in new and different ways)

4. Invite the children to examine a sealed box and ask them to discuss the different ways they could open the box. (Encouraging the children to think of and try multiple ways to solve a problem)

5. Invite the children to examine a sealed box and ask them to talk about what might be inside the box. (Using materials in new and different ways)

6. Place some boxes in the block corner and invite the children to use them with blocks, miniature people, or animal figures. (Using materials in new and different ways)

7. Supply the children with cereal boxes and invite them to create hats, masks, or anything else they wish to. (Open-ended art experiences)

8. Challenge the children to find ways to move a box without touching the box with their hands. (Movement, Encouraging the children to think of and try multiple ways to solve a problem)

9. Ask the children to use various size boxes as drums. Play some music and invite the children to be the percussion section of the orchestra. (Music)

10. Put some boxes in the sandbox, and invite the children to use them. (Using materials in new and different ways)

11. Invite the children to paint on corrugated cardboard from a box. (Open-ended art experiences)

Part II

Themes and Activities for Hands-On Learning

4

BALLS

Balls of all types are a lot of fun to play with, and studying them (working with them) provides a great opportunity to encourage physical activity. You and the children can throw, catch, bounce, roll, or kick balls as well as hit them with bats, golf clubs, pool cues, ping-pong paddles, and tennis racquets. Whatever you do, have a ball!

HELP CHILDREN DISCOVER

1. Balls are fun to play with.

2. Balls are made of different materials.

3. Balls are usually round. However, a football is an ellipsoid shaped ball.

4. Balls come in different sizes.

5. Balls can be light (ping-pong ball) or heavy (bowling ball).

6. Balls can be solid or inflatable (filled with air).

7. Balls can be thrown through hoops, over nets, or into nets.

8. In sports, certain balls are hit with special objects such as bats or paddles.

9. Some foods are prepared to look like balls, such as meatballs, melon balls, or popcorn balls.

10. When balls are attached to objects, they help the objects move or rotate more easily. Examples are chairs, carts, and ball bearings in bicycle pedals and wheels.

LITERACY

1. Create a recipe chart, and invite the children to follow the directions to help make meatballs, peanut butter balls, or cheese balls.

2. Invite the children to play a game. Ask the children to sit on the floor in a circle. Then, sing or chant the phrase, "I roll the ball to someone wearing red" and roll a ball to a child wearing something red. Then, sing or chant, "And someone

wearing red rolls the ball back to me." Do this with several different colors. To keep the children attentive, try to alternate who you roll the ball to, rather than going around the circle in order. You can also use letters instead of colors. For example, "I roll the ball to Barry, whose name starts with B" or "I roll the ball to Juanita, who has an n in her name."

3. To play another "roll the ball" game with the children, arrange a number of items in a semicircle on the floor—for example, a block, a doll, a hat, and a shoe. Tape the letters of the alphabet that correspond to the first letters of the items on the floor onto soft rubber or foam balls (one letter per ball). Place the balls in a bag. Invite the children to reach into the bag, pull out a ball, identify the letter taped to the ball, and then roll that ball to the item with the corresponding initial letter.

4. Create a letter recognition game. Put some water in the sensory table. Use permanent markers to print letters on ping-pong balls and place them in the water. Give a child a small aquarium fish net and encourage the child to scoop out a ping-pong ball and identify the letter printed on it. To make this activity simpler, use colors instead of letters. To make this activity more challenging, encourage the children to fish for specific letters—for example, "Go fish for a B," or "Go fish for the first letter of your name or a friend's name."

5. Create a game where the children match an assortment of balls to the sports equipment that they are used with. For example, baseball to bat, tennis ball to tennis racquet, and basketball to hoop.

6. On index cards, print the letters found on an assortment of balls. For example, the letters W-I-L-S-O-N are printed on some soccer balls. Print one letter per card. Give each of the children an index card and challenge them to find the corresponding letter on a ball.

7. On the playground, wet down different balls. Invite the children to roll the balls on a paved surface, and notice the different patterns that the balls make. This could be done indoors using paint and paper. To make this activity more challenging, out of the sight of the children, roll balls dipped in one color of paint on paper to create patterns, Then, ask the children to examine the balls and guess which ball made which pattern.

8. Invite the children to sort pompoms by color.

9. Put ice cream scoops in the sandbox, dampen the sand, and encourage the children to make mud pie balls. Encourage the children to talk about their creations.

10. Bring in balls made of twine, yarn, or rubber bands for the children to handle and discuss.

11. To encourage dramatic play, make a pretend microphone by cutting a slit in a tennis ball and mounting it on a small stick or tongue depressor. The children can pretend to be sports commentators, singers, disc jockeys, or anything else they may think of.

12. Place an assortment of balls in a large bag. Invite a child to reach in the bag, pull out a ball, and identify the ball. Then, ask all the children to look for an item that begins with the same initial letter sound as the ball. For example, if a child pulls out a golf ball the children would look for things that begin with the letter G. They could look for a glove, or something that is green. For a baseball, they would look for things that begin with the letter B—for example, a bag or a boot. To make this activity simpler, place items or pictures of items with the same initial sound as the balls in the bag on a nearby table. Then, ask the children to identify the item that has the same initial letter as the ball from the items on the table. To make this activity more challenging, you could tape different letters of the alphabet to the balls in the bag and ask the children to look for items that begin with the same letter that is taped on the balls.

13. Place an assortment of balls on the floor. Discuss with the children words (adjectives) that they could use to describe the different balls, or how the balls are alike and how they are different.

MATHEMATICS

1. Challenge the children to bounce a large ball. Count aloud the number of times each child bounces the ball.

2. Place a collection of different-size balls on the floor and invite the children to order the balls by size from the smallest to the largest.

3. Give the children a collection of balls, and challenge them to arrange the balls by weight.

4. Invite the children to throw a ball on the playground, mark where it lands, and then measure how far each child threw the ball. The distance a ball has traveled can also be measured after letting the children kick a ball or hit it with a golf club or bat. Careful adult supervision is required when children are using sports equipment.

5. Put tennis balls in a clear plastic container and ask the children to estimate how many balls are in the container. Then, with the children, count the balls. This activity can be made more challenging by increasing the size of the container (thereby increasing its capacity) or by using smaller balls such as ping-pong balls.

6. Invite the children to color in the outline of large-size numbers that have been written on a piece of construction paper. Then, help the children cut out the numbers and tape them onto their shirts so they resemble football, baseball, or soccer team shirts. To make this activity more challenging, ask the children to write a number of their choice on the paper and then cut it out. After the children have their numbers taped to their shirts, challenge them to line up in numerical order before going out on the playground to play with balls.

7. Create a game. Place a bowl that is filled with tokens on a table. On the floor, place a few different-size boxes with the numbers "1," "2," and "3" written on them. Write one number on each box. Place a piece of tape on the floor a few

feet away from the boxes. Challenge the children to stand on the tape and toss a ping-pong or other small ball into one of the boxes. Then, ask the children to select the same number of tokens as the number that is written on the box that the ball landed in. After each child collects six tokens, the game is over. To make this activity more challenging, write higher numbers on the boxes or ask the children to collect more than six tokens.

8. Encourage the children to make different-size balls with play dough, and then ask them to arrange the balls from the smallest to the largest.

9. Place a collection of different-size balls on the floor and challenge the children to use a piece of string or ribbon, or a tape measure to measure the circumference of each ball.

10. Create a target toss game. Tape pieces of paper with different geometric shapes drawn on them to a suitable location. Challenge the children to hit the triangle, square, or circle target with a soft sponge ball. This activity can be done indoors or outdoors.

11. Create a simple bingo game using ping-pong balls. Prepare a game board by dividing a piece of construction paper into six equal parts. In each section of the board, write a number. Write the corresponding numbers on ping-pong balls. Write one number on each ping-pong ball. Give each child a board and place a bowl of tokens nearby. Put the ping-pong balls in a container. Have a child reach into the container and pick a ping-pong ball. Ask the children to identify the number on the ping-pong ball and then look for that number on their game board and cover it with a token. The game is over when all the numbers on the board are covered with a token. To add variety you could draw a smiley face on a ping-pong ball. When a child picks the ball with the smiley face, he gets to choose the number. To make this activity more challenging, you could print dots on the board instead of numbers, or you could use higher numbers. If you tape the numbers to the ping-pong balls, you could then remove the numbers and create new games using letters or shapes. Simply create new boards and tape the corresponding letters or shapes to the ping-pong balls.

12. Invite the children to handle a beach ball and then challenge them to count the number of different colors on the beach ball.

SCIENCE

1. Invite the children to roll different balls down an incline board or the playground slide. Encourage the children to observe and comment on the varying speeds of the different balls. After the children have experimented for a while, if possible change the angle of incline of the board.

2. Create an opportunity for the children to develop their observation skills and speculate about cause and effect. Do not announce what will happen—just let the children observe. Place a ping-pong ball or golf ball in the middle

of a table. Does it stay still, or does it roll? Then, put a small piece of cardboard under one of the table legs. Will this affect the ball? How? Next, put a larger piece of cardboard under a leg of the table so that it is tilted, then ask the children to speculate about what might happen to the ball. Results may vary depending on the size and weight of the ball. Invite the children to make comparisons. For instance, a golf ball may roll faster (more readily) than a basketball or ping-pong ball. You could also give the children a tray with a ball on it and encourage them to experiment by tilting the tray at different angles to see how the ball moves.

3. Invite the children to play with a beach ball. Inflate the ball completely and ask the children to roll it. After a while, let a small amount of air out of the ball and ask the children to speculate about what might happen when there is less air in the ball. Invite the children to roll the ball again. Continue to slowly deflate the ball, each time inviting the children to speculate, roll the ball, and then observe. Keep in mind that the purpose of this activity is to invite speculation and observation rather than to have the children just guess the correct answer.

4. Out of the sight of the children, bounce a ball on the floor or table. Challenge the children to identify the ball by the sound it makes when bounced. Repeat this activity with different types of balls. Be sure to include Styrofoam balls.

5. Put water and different kinds of balls in the sensory table. Ask the children to observe which balls sink and which balls float.

6. Put a ball in a feely box and invite the children to see if they can identify the ball by touch. This is a good opportunity to use vocabulary such as fuzzy, hard, or bumpy.

7. Invite the children to use a magnifying glass to get a closer look at the different surfaces of a collection of balls. Be sure to include a tennis ball and a ball of twine or yarn.

8. Label four tennis balls using a different label for each ball. With the children, roll two of the tennis balls in water and leave two of the balls dry. Then, place one of the wet tennis balls and a dry tennis ball in the freezer. After an hour, remove the two balls from the freezer. Ask the children to observe carefully as the balls that were in the freezer are dropped or bounced on the floor. For comparison purposes, also bounce the dry and wet tennis balls that were not placed in the freezer. Discuss with the children their observations about how high the different balls bounce. Leave the balls out of the freezer and try bouncing them again in an hour or two.

9. Invite the children to move balls by blowing on them. Place a ping-pong ball, a golf ball, and a basketball on a table or the floor. Ask the children to speculate about which one they can move the farthest and why. Does blowing through a straw make it easier?

10. If the weather cooperates, invite the children to make snowballs. Encourage the children to make different-size snowballs, and then bring them indoors to observe what happens.

11. Use a jumbo-size flexible straw and a ping-pong ball to illustrate that we cannot see airflow, but we can feel it and use it to move things. Place the long end of a flexible straw in your mouth and bend up the short end so it resembles a pipe. Then, blow through the straw and ask the children to feel the flow of air. Then, hold a ping-pong ball just above the end of the straw, and blow through the straw. If you then let go of the ball, your stream of air should be able to support the ping-pong ball a few inches above the straw. The ball will appear to hang in mid air. Encourage the children to experiment by blocking the stream of air. You could also try to repeat this experiment with other balls. Encourage the children to speculate about whether the stream of air coming through the straw will be able to support the other balls, and if not, why not?

12. Invite the children to closely examine a whistle. They should see a small ball inside the whistle. Blow the whistle and encourage the children to listen to the sound that it makes. Then, use the tines of a fork to hold the ball inside the whistle still. Blow the whistle again. What effect does holding the ball still have on the sound of the whistle? If possible, open a whistle, remove the ball, and reseal the whistle. Then, blow on the whistle without a ball inside it and listen to the sound that it makes.

SOCIAL STUDIES

1. Ask the children to bring in a ball from home and discuss who uses the ball. You may get anything from bowling, tennis, and soccer balls to bocce, medicine, or beach balls.

2. In China, palm-size heavy stone or metal balls called Qigong balls are used as part of an exercise routine. Invite someone in to demonstrate the use of these balls.

3. Arrange a visit to a local high school to observe a soccer, baseball, basketball, or football team practice.

4. Invite a family dog to class that likes to play with balls. Ask the children to observe as the dog catches or retrieves the ball.

☺☺☺☺☺☺☺☺☺☺☺☺☺☺
Invite the children who do not have pets to talk about a pretend or imaginary pet.
☺☺☺☺☺☺☺☺☺☺☺☺☺☺

5. Discuss pets with the children. Ask the children if their pets like to play with balls. Invite the children who do not have pets to talk about a pretend or imaginary pet.

6. Encourage the children to cooperate. Ask two children to face one another, and then place a large beach ball between them. Ask the children to move from Point A to Point B without dropping the ball or using their hands.

7. Invite the children to help prepare a melon ball salad. Invite some of the people who work in the building to come join you for this specially prepared snack.

8. Visit a sporting goods store and look at all the different types of balls.

9. Challenge the children to cooperate by trying to roll a heavy medicine ball from Point A to Point B.

10. Invite someone to the classroom to demonstrate how to juggle balls.

PHYSICAL DEVELOPMENT

1. Invite the children to crumple paper or aluminum foil to make balls.

2. Challenge the children to balance a golf ball on a tablespoon and see how far they can walk without dropping it.

3. Invite the children to roll or hit ping-pong balls into small cups or boxes turned on their side. Give the children a pencil or rhythm stick to hit the ping-pong balls. This can be done at a table or on the floor.

4. Invite the children to try and toss different balls into a basket or box.

5. Encourage the children to toss, catch, bounce, roll, and kick balls.

6. Challenge the children to try to bowl. Set up a "bowling alley" using a medium-size soccer or rubber ball as the bowling ball. Use empty plastic bottles as bowling pins. If you put a little sand in the bottles, they will be more stable. To make this activity simpler, use larger-size balls and larger-size plastic bottles.

7. Challenge the children to try and sit on large balls. To make this activity more challenging, ask the children to try to move from Point A to Point B while remaining seated on a large ball.

8. Place a ball on a parachute and encourage the children to cooperate and move the ball around the parachute. This activity can be made more challenging by using more than one ball, or by asking the children to get the ball to fall through the hole in the center of the parachute.

9. Suspend a Wiffle ball in a doorway or other suitable location. Encourage the children to jump up and try to tap the ball.

10. Place a target on the floor. You could use a pie tin, or tape a 9×12 piece of paper to the floor. Place a piece of tape on the floor a few feet away. Encourage the children to stand on the tape and toss a ball onto the target.

CREATIVITY

1. Invite the children to create a new ball game.

2. Discuss a problem involving a beach ball and encourage the children to think of different ways to solve the problem. Pretend you are going to drive to the beach or a pool in a car. The car is crowded with people, a dog, toys, blankets, an umbrella, and a picnic basket. You have a large inflated beach ball that you want to take to the beach, but there is not enough room for it in the car. What can you

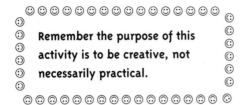

Remember the purpose of this activity is to be creative, not necessarily practical.

do? Try to get the children to go beyond the possibly obvious answer of letting air out of the ball. Remember the purpose of this activity is to be creative, not necessarily practical.

3. Discuss with the children the different ways balls can be used other than in connection with sports activities. For example, balls can be juggled for entertainment, or rolled around on, as in a ball crawl, which is an enclosed area that is filled with colored plastic balls. There is even an exercise chair that consists of a large balance ball set onto the frame of a desk chair.

4. Invite the children to decorate or design their own balls. For example, tape ribbons or colored pieces of paper to balls, or use markers to make designs on ping-pong balls.

5. Invite the children to create a dish for snack or lunch that can be shaped like a ball. For example, ice cream scoops can be used to mold tuna fish salad or potato salad.

6. Invite the children to dip a golf ball in paint, put it in a box with a piece of paper on the bottom of it, and roll the ball around to make patterns.

7. Cut slits in balls so that they can be used as puppet heads. Invite the children to decorate the balls, and encourage them to put the balls on their fingers and put on a puppet show.

5
Cotton Balls

Despite the fact that cotton balls do not come in different shapes or materials they can still offer a variety of interesting activities. Soft, fuzzy, inexpensive, and easy to find, cotton balls will be a fun topic to explore.

HELP CHILDREN DISCOVER

1. Cotton balls are soft.
2. Cotton balls are round.
3. Cotton balls are lightweight.
4. Cotton balls come in different sizes.
5. Cotton balls are made from cotton.
6. Cotton balls can be used for many different purposes.

LITERACY

1. Print a letter on a piece of construction paper. Put double-stick tape on the letter. Invite the children to place cotton balls on the letter and create a soft cotton ball letter. To make this activity more challenging, print the children's names instead of a letter.

2. Place one of the cotton ball letters from the previous activity in a feely box. Challenge the children to reach in the box and try to identify the letter using their sense of touch. Start with simple letters—for example, O or T.

3. Place a cotton ball, ping-pong ball, and basketball on a table for the children to handle. Discuss with the children how the balls are similar to one another. Then, discuss how the balls are different from one another.

4. Invite the children to make and use paper bag puppets. Put out a generous supply of cotton balls for decoration.

5. Tape or place a few large pieces of different colored construction paper on a table or on the floor. Ask a child to stand with her back to the pieces of paper. Give her a cotton ball and ask her to toss the cotton ball over her shoulder onto a piece of paper. Then, ask each child to find three items in the room that are the same color as the piece of paper that the cotton ball landed on. To make this activity more challenging, ask the child to identify the color. You could also use printed letters instead of colored construction paper, and then ask the child to identify the letter the cotton ball landed on, and say a word that starts with the same sound as that letter.

6. Encourage the children to use cotton balls as a prop to create a story.

7. Give each child a cotton ball to hold. Then, ask the children to suggest words (adjectives) or phrases that describe a cotton ball. For example, "soft," "fuzzy," or "like a cloud." You could also ask the children for words and phrases that they would not use to describe a cotton ball—for example, "heavy," or "hard as a rock."

8. Invite the children to dab cotton balls in paint and make designs on a piece of paper. Discuss with the children the colors that they used, and the designs that they made.

9. To encourage dramatic play, place some cotton balls along with medical equipment and materials, such as a stethoscope and band-aids, in the dramatic play area.

10. Invite the children to make masks. Suggest they use cotton balls for decorations.

11. Give each child a cotton ball. Ask the children to listen carefully as they rub the cotton ball against their ear. Talk about what the sounds remind them of.

MATHEMATICS

1. Place a large number of cotton balls in a shoebox and replace the lid. Make a hole in one end of the box large enough for a child's hand to fit through. Challenge the children to reach in the box and see how many cotton balls they can pick up in one hand and remove from the box. Then, count the cotton balls with the children.

2. Create a game using a spinner. Put a bowl of cotton balls in the center of a table. Give each child a piece of paper with an outline drawn on it—for example, the outline of a snowman, a hill, or a cat. Ask each child to use the spinner, identify the number, and take the corresponding number of cotton balls. The child can then place or paste her cotton balls on the outline drawn on her piece of paper. The children may prefer blank pieces of paper to create their own designs using the cotton balls. This activity can be made more challenging by using higher numbers on the spinner or by using a pair of dice instead of a spinner.

3. Place a large number of cotton balls on the floor or on a table. Invite the children to use the cotton balls to create different geometric shapes. For example, show the children a piece of paper with a triangle drawn on it. Then, challenge the children to use the cotton balls to make a shape that matches the geometric shape drawn on the piece of paper. This activity can be made more challenging by asking the children to use the cotton balls to make a geometric shape, such as a triangle, without showing them a drawing of the shape.

4. Show the children an empty cup. Ask the children to guess how many cotton balls it would take to fill the cup. Ask the children to count as they place the cotton balls one by one into the cup until it is filled. This activity can be made more challenging by using a larger container, which would require more cotton balls.

5. Ask a child to put three cotton balls on one side of a balance scale and the same number of nails, pebbles, or other items on the other side of the scale. Encourage the children to compare the weight of the different items.

6. Place a large bowl of cotton balls on a table. Use the cotton balls to create a pattern—for example, three vertical cotton balls and two horizontal cotton balls. Then, challenge the children to match your pattern. This activity can be made more challenging by using more cotton balls. You could also ask the children to look at the pattern for a moment, cover it with a piece of paper, and challenge the children to replicate the pattern from memory. Be sure you let the children create patterns for you to match as well.

7. Create a cotton ball variation of shuffleboard. Use masking tape or washable paint to make a square on one end of a tabletop. Divide the square into four zones, and write a different number in each zone. Draw a line at the other end of the table. Give a child a pencil and ask her to stand by the line. Invite the child to place a cotton ball anywhere on the line, and use the pencil to hit the cotton ball into one of the zones. When the cotton ball lands in a zone, the child gets to select the corresponding number of tokens. The game is over when each child has collected the predetermined number of tokens. This activity can be made more challenging by writing higher numbers in the zones.

8. Give each child a piece of construction paper with a line drawn on it. Invite the children to place or paste cotton balls on the line on their piece of paper, and then count how many cotton balls they used. This activity can be made more challenging by drawing a longer line or using more than one line. If the children use paste, have a supply of damp paper towels handy for sticky little fingers.

If the children use paste, have a supply of damp paper towels handy for sticky little fingers.

9. Invite the children to create their own tactile counting book. Using one index card for each number, write the numbers 0 to 5. Ask the children to paste the corresponding number of cotton balls on each page. The children can also decorate the pages. When done, fasten the cards together. This activity can be made more challenging by writing higher numbers.

10. Use cotton balls and index cards to create a tactile domino set. Invite the children to play with the dominoes. This activity can be made simpler by limiting the dominoes you make to less than five dots.

11. Challenge the children to see how far they can throw a cotton ball. Invite the children to measure the distance they threw the cotton ball.

12. Place an assortment of different-size cotton balls on a table. Invite the children to sort the cotton balls by size.

SCIENCE

1. With the children, dip a few cotton balls in water and squeeze a little of the water out of the cotton balls. Put the cotton balls on a plate or piece of aluminum foil and place them in the freezer. For comparison purposes, also place some dry cotton balls in the freezer. Encourage the children to speculate about how the cotton balls will look and feel after they have been in the freezer for a few hours. After a few hours, remove the cotton balls and ask the children to

talk about how they look. Then, ask the children to touch the cotton balls and talk about how the cotton balls feel. Encourage the children to compare the cotton balls that were dipped in water and those that were kept dry.

2. Give each child a cotton ball. Encourage the children to rub the cotton ball on their hair, face, lips, arm, and leg. Discuss with the children how the cotton ball feels on each part of their body. Does it feel the same or different?

3. Give the children two rhythm sticks. Cover one end of one of the sticks with cotton balls and secure with tape. Invite the children to tap both sticks on different surfaces. Ask the children to compare the sounds made by the sticks.

4. Gather a collection of assorted items such as small blocks, large nails, ribbons, spoons, plastic cups, crayons, pie tins, and cotton balls. Invite the children to drop the items on a table or uncarpeted floor. Encourage the children to listen to the sounds the different items make when they are dropped. Then, suggest to the children that they drop the same items on a small area of the floor that has been covered with cotton balls. Encourage the children to speculate about how the sounds might be different, and then ask the children to listen to the sounds that are made when the items are dropped on cotton balls.

5. Put water in the sensory table. Give the children cotton balls and encourage them to experiment with the cotton balls in the water. Discuss with the children what happens to the cotton balls after a period of time.

6. Use tape to secure a round pencil or marker to a tabletop. Place a tongue depressor at a right angle across the top of the pencil so that one end of the tongue depressor rests on the table. It should resemble a miniature seesaw. Invite the children to place a cotton ball on the end of the tongue depressor that is touching the table. Then, with a quick firm motion, press down on the other end of the tongue depressor. In this activity, the children are using a lever, which is a simple machine, as a miniature catapult. This activity should be carefully supervised and done only with cotton balls: flying projectiles can be dangerous.

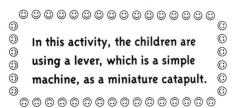

In this activity, the children are using a lever, which is a simple machine, as a miniature catapult.

7. Invite the children to use a magnifying glass to closely inspect cotton balls.

8. Out of the sight of the children, dip cotton balls in various scents such as vanilla, liquid soap, or oil of wintergreen. Prepare two cotton balls for each scent. Place each cotton ball in a small cup and challenge the children to use their sense of smell to match the cups by scent.

9. Create an activity for the children to use their sense of touch. Place some cotton balls, a nail, ribbon, piece of fabric, and other items in a feely box. Challenge the children to reach in the box and remove only the cotton balls.

10. Invite the children to place cotton balls in clear plastic cups and then moisten the cotton balls with water. Ask the children to put a lima bean seed between the wall of the cup and the cotton balls, so the seed is clearly visible.

Have enough lima bean seeds available so the children can put two to three seeds in each cup. Place the cups in a dark area, such as in a closet. Keep the cotton balls moist but not soggy. Ask the children to check the seeds daily for changes in the appearance of the lima beans. After a few days, roots should appear. Later, the stem and leaves will emerge from the lima beans and begin to grow. The plants can then be moved to a sunny area of the room. When the plants become large, they will need to be put in soil. Encourage the children to observe the plants and their growth daily. This activity provides an opportunity to talk about the growth sequence of a lima bean. You could also discuss the growth sequence of other living things such as people, dogs, or butterflies.

> This activity provides an opportunity to talk about the growth sequence of a lima bean. You could also discuss the growth sequence of other living things such as people, dogs, or butterflies.

11. Gather together several small items such as rocks, crayons, small toys, and cotton balls. Place the items on a table and challenge the children to blow on the items to see if they can be moved using only air.

12. Ask a child to ring a bell that has a clapper inside it. Encourage the children to listen carefully to the sound that is made. Then, ask the child to stuff a few cotton balls inside the bell. If it is a large bell, help the child tape cotton balls around the clapper. Ask the children to listen carefully as someone tries to ring the bell again. Discuss with the children the difference in the sounds that the bell made with and without the cotton balls.

SOCIAL STUDIES

1. Invite the children to cooperate with one another by helping to decorate a bulletin board in the classroom. The children could glue cotton balls randomly onto a large piece of paper and call it a snow storm, or you could draw a snowman, cat, tree, hill, clouds, birds, or field of dandelions for the children to decorate with cotton balls.

2. Ask the children if they have cotton balls at home, where they are kept, and how they are used.

3. Visit the cosmetics department of a large department store and see a demonstration of how cotton balls are used with makeup.

4. Arrange for a local actor and actress to visit the class and demonstrate how they put on and take off makeup, or try to visit backstage at a local community theatre when the actors are putting on makeup for a dress rehearsal. Stay and watch part of the rehearsal.

5. Invite a nurse or dental hygienist to class and ask him to talk about the use of cotton balls.

6. Visit a nail salon, beauty parlor, or barber shop and watch a manicurist at work.

7. Encourage the children to take care of a plant. Ask the children to use a cotton ball to gently dust the leaves of the plant.

PHYSICAL DEVELOPMENT

1. Make a line of cotton balls on the floor and challenge the children to jump over it. To make this activity more challenging, use several rows of cotton balls.

2. Ask the children to separate out individual cotton balls from a large package of them.

3. Place a cotton ball on the floor and challenge a child to blow the cotton ball from Point A to Point B. A variation on this activity would be for the child to blow through a straw to move the cotton ball.

4. Invite the children to play catch with cotton balls.

5. Challenge the children to try to tear cotton balls into smaller pieces.

6. Challenge the children to pick up cotton balls using a tweezers or spring clothespin, and place them in a cup.

7. Ask the children to place a cotton ball on a large spoon. Then, challenge the children to move from Point A to Point B without dropping the cotton ball. You can make this activity more challenging by using a smaller spoon or asking the children to walk backward or slide sideways to get from Point A to Point B.

8. Place several cotton balls on a parachute or a sheet and invite the children to make the cotton balls move.

9. Give the children a supply of cotton balls and suggest they use them to clean some small toys.

CREATIVITY

1. Invite the children to draw with chalk on black paper and then rub the paper with cotton balls to make a design. Afterward, look at the designs and discuss with the children what the different designs remind them of—for example, a snowstorm, fog, an ice-cream cone, or clouds.

2. Place several cotton balls on a table for the children to handle. Then, discuss with the children the different ways that they could use cotton balls.

3. Challenge the children to create a new game using cotton balls.

4. Invite the children to create a design on construction paper using glue or paste. Ask the children to place cotton balls on the glue to create a collage. Have available sandpaper, ribbons, or other items for the children to use as part of their collage.

5. Pose a problem to the children. If you do not have any cotton balls, what could you use in place of them?

6. Discuss with the children their ideas on how to make cotton balls better.

7. Add cotton balls to the block corner.

8. To stimulate dramatic play, add cotton balls to the kitchen area of the housekeeping corner.

6

Hats

Hats can be symbols of status. They can communicate loyalty to a team, group, or place. Hats can indicate a profession, or they can just be decorative, funny, or playful. Hats provide important protection from sun, rain, and cold. Specially designed hard hats are used for protection by baseball players, firefighters, bicyclists, and construction workers. This theme provides a good opportunity to reinforce nonsexist attitudes about career choices. Positive feelings about cultural diversity can also be reinforced: people all over the world wear hats or some type of headwear. Children will enjoy handling and trying on hats as well as exploring all the things that they can represent.

> This theme provides a good opportunity to reinforce nonsexist attitudes about career choices. Positive feelings about cultural diversity can also be reinforced: people all over the world wear hats or some type of headwear.

HELP CHILDREN DISCOVER

1. Hats are made of different materials.

2. Hats come in different sizes.

3. Hats can be worn for fun or for a special reason.

4. Hats can be part of a uniform or related to a job (police officer, nurse, chef).

5. Some hats are designed to protect people (fire helmets, hard hats, motorcycle helmets).

6. Some hats help keep us warm. Some hats protect us from rain or sun.

7. Special hats are designed for sports (baseball, football, hockey, bicycling, and spelunking).

LITERACY

1. On a table, place several different hats. In a box, place items that people who wear the hats might use. For example, sun hat (plastic sunglasses, beach shovel,

pail), nurse's cap (band-aid, cotton ball, empty plastic prescription container), police officer's hat (whistle, white gloves), baseball cap (baseball, baseball glove), shower cap (bar of soap, washcloth, sponge), chef's hat (large spoon, oven mitt, spatula, frying pan). Invite the children to reach in the box, remove an item, and then place it next to the hat they think it belongs with. Discuss with the children the choices that they made and the reasons for their choices. To make this activity more challenging, add some items that could be used by several people—for example, a pen, paper, book, or keys.

2. Ask the children to bring in baseball caps that have letters on them. Encourage the children to look for letters on the caps that match the letters in their names.

3. Place a collection of baseball caps with letters on them on a table. Prepare index cards with letters printed on them. Print one letter on each index card. Ask a child to pick an index card, identify the letter printed on it, and then find a baseball cap that has the same letter. To make this activity more challenging, ask the child to name an object that begins with the same letter that is printed on the index card. To make this activity simpler, limit the number of letters by preparing fewer index cards or by printing letters on a die instead of on an index card.

4. To encourage dramatic play, set up a hat store in the dramatic play area. Try to have unbreakable mirrors available for the children to admire themselves.

5. Invite the children to sort a collection of hats. Discuss with the children different criteria for sorting—for example, hats for work, hats for fun, hats for protection; or soft hats and hard hats.

6. Place several hats on a table and challenge the children to sort the hats by color.

7. Design a letter recognition game. Place a collection of several different hats on a table—for example, firefighter's helmet, baseball cap, nurse's cap, and police officer's hat. On a piece of paper placed next to each hat, write the occupation of the person who wears that hat—for example, nurse or firefighter. Prepare a stack of index cards on which you have printed the first letter in each of the words that you wrote on the pieces of paper. Print one letter on each index card. Invite the children to pick a card and then match the letter that is printed on the card to the first letter of the occupation written next to each hat. For example, F for Firefighter, C for Chef, N for Nurse. If the children notice a corresponding letter that is not the initial letter of the word, that is good, too. For example, the letter f in Chef. This activity can be made simpler by decreasing the number of hats used, or it can be made more challenging by increasing the number of letters you print on index cards, using upper and lowercase letters, or printing the entire word.

8. Collect all the children's hats and put them in a pile on a table. Challenge the children to find their hat. To make this activity more challenging, hold up a hat

and ask the children to identify the owner. Before doing this activity, attach temporary labels to each child's hat.

9. Put a top hat in the dramatic play corner and encourage the children to do magic tricks.

10. Use hats as a prop when telling a story. For example, when telling the story of the Three Billy Goats Gruff, put on a hat to represent the troll when you talk about the troll. Use three different hats—small, medium, and large—to represent the goats when you talk about them.

11. Read the book *Caps for Sale by* Esphyr Slobodkina. Invite the children to dramatize the story.

12. Discuss with the children if anyone in their family wears hats. Talk about when and where they wear hats.

13. Place scraps of colored paper in a hat that is turned upside down. Invite a child to close his eyes and reach into the hat to pick out a piece of paper. Then, challenge the children to go find two items that are the same color as the piece of colored paper that was selected. To make this activity more challenging, you could print the color word instead of using pieces of colored paper.

14. With the children, write a letter to a high school principal. Ask permission to visit the school to see a football or baseball team practice session in order to see the special hats that are worn as protection.

15. Create a story-telling corner. Provide a chair and a special hat that a child can put on to indicate she has a story she would like to tell.

MATHEMATICS

1. Use a tape measure and measure the circumference of each child's head. Create a graph of the head sizes of the children. Discuss with the children the fact that different people wear different size hats because they have different size heads.

2. Invite the children to order a collection of hats by size. Look for labels indicating size on the inside of hats. Be sure to note the use of fractions.

3. Invite the children to carry different hats across the room. Ask the children if they notice any difference in the weight of the hats. Try to have available everything from a baseball cap to a firefighter's helmet. Or you could place an assortment of hats on a table and ask the children to order the hats from the lightest to the heaviest.

4. With the children, create a graph of the different colors of the hats that the children wear to school.

5. Out of the sight of the children, trace the shape of some hats on different pieces of paper. Try to include a cone shaped wizard's hat, a three-corner hat, a

beanie cap, and any other hats you choose. Place the hats on a table along with the traced outlines of the hats. Challenge the children to match the hats to the traced outlines.

6. Challenge the children to see how many baseball caps they can stack. Then, with the children, count the caps in the stack.

7. Create a game using a spinner. Make a simple paper crown hat for each child. Invite the children to decorate their hats by playing a game. Ask the children to use the spinner, identify the number, and then select the corresponding number of items from an assortment of stickers, stars, or strips of colored paper. They can then glue the items onto their hats. Have plenty of supplies on hand so the children can have as many turns as they want and decorate their hats to their hearts' content. This game can be made simpler by having fewer numbers on the spinner or by using only small numbers.

> Have plenty of supplies on hand so the children can have as many turns as they want and decorate their hats to their hearts' content.

8. Collect an assortment of sun hats and invite the children to measure and compare the different sizes of the brims.

9. Invite the children to closely inspect a baseball cap, which can be adjusted to different sizes using an adjustable back-snap tab strap. Ask the children to determine whether they need to use the first, second, or third hole for the hat to fit them properly. Then, ask the children to compare that with the adjustment that an adult requires.

10. Invite the children to play a hat toss game. Have available a bowl of tokens. Use tape on the floor to delineate different zones. Write a number in each zone. This could look like a simple shuffleboard or hopscotch court. Invite a child to toss a hat into one of the zones from a short distance away. Ask the child to identify the number written in the zone and then select the corresponding number of tokens from the bowl. When the child accumulates ten tokens, the game is over. This game can be made simpler by using lower numbers in the zones or by completing the game when the child has five tokens. You could also put dots in the zones instead of writing numbers.

11. Invite the children to examine a collection of hats. Ask the children to count the number of different colors that are on each hat. Challenge the children to find the hat with the most (highest number of) different colors.

12. Place a few baseballs in the crown of an upside down baseball cap. Encourage the children to estimate how many balls are in the cap. Count the number of balls with the children. To make this activity more challenging, use ping-pong balls or golf balls.

SCIENCE

1. Collect an assortment of hats made from different materials. Invite the children to use a magnifying glass to get a close look at the different materials from which the hats were made.

2. Take several different style hats outdoors on a sunny day. Ask the children to try the hats on and then decide which hat is best to wear on a sunny day. Discuss with the children their reasons for selecting the hat that they chose. Do the same activity for hats that are used in cold weather. Ask the children to decide which hat they think would be best to wear in cold weather. Encourage the children to notice and discuss things like the materials used, air vents, and earflaps to protect the ears.

3. Invite the children to look in a mirror as they remove tight-fitting knit or polyester hats from their heads. Discuss with the children what they saw and felt when they removed the hats. The static electricity caused by the friction of removing the hats should make the children's hair stand on end. The children may also see sparks as a result of the static electricity they generated. You could also ask the children to rub an inflated balloon on their hats and then place the balloon on their chest or against a wall. The static electricity caused by rubbing the balloon on the hats should cause the balloon to temporarily stick to different surfaces. This activity works best in cool, dry weather.

4. Out of the sight of the children, put a hat in a bag. Then, invite the children to reach in and touch the hat. Ask the children to describe the hat and guess which hat is in the bag using only their sense of touch.

5. Invite the children to tap hats made of different materials with a pencil and listen to the different sounds that are made.

6. On a table, place a collection of pictures of different places and weather conditions. For example, use pictures of a sunny beach, snow on top of a mountain, or a rainy day at sea. Give the children a collection of hats, and ask them to match the proper hat to each picture.

7. Position a sheet so that a child can stand behind it. For example, you could attach the sheet to two easels that are a few feet apart. Place a source of light behind the sheet. Invite two of the children to put on hats and then stand behind the sheet and in front of the source of light to create shadows. Challenge the other children to identify the child who is standing on the left and the child who is standing on the right by looking at the shadows that the two children cast. Encourage the children to experiment with shadows by moving toward or away from the sheet, or moving toward or away from the source of light.

8. In a darkened or dimly lit area of the room, give the children flashlights and ask them to shine the flashlights on a firefighter's helmet and some other hats. Discuss with the children why some hats have reflective tape on them.

9. Place an assortment of hats on a table and ask the children to order the hats from the softest to the hardest. Discuss with the children why some hats need to be hard.

10. Place a few waterproof hats and some washable knit hats in the sensory table. Invite the children to pour water over the hats and observe them.

SOCIAL STUDIES

1. Ask the children's families to send to school a special hat. Suggest that the hat could be part of a uniform, traditional costume, a hat for a special occasion, a lucky hat, or just a favorite hat. Encourage the children to talk about the hats and who uses them.

2. Ask the children's families if they would like to come to school to talk about or demonstrate any traditional dances that involve hats. For example, someone could show the children how to dance the *Jarabe Tapatio,* which is the national dance of Mexico. It is known in English as the Mexican Hat Dance.

3. Visit a sporting goods store and look at the different kinds of hats. Be sure to look at hats designed for spelunkers and scuba divers.

4. Organize a happy un-birthday party. Invite the children to make party hats. Discuss with the children what they usually do to celebrate their birthdays.

5. Invite a school crossing guard to come in and show the children the hat and rain hat that she wears when working outdoors.

6. Visit the hat department in a department store.

7. Visit the school cafeteria or a fast-food restaurant. Notice the special hats that food handlers wear and discuss why they wear hats.

8. Invite the children to create their own hats and then wear them in a parade. You could have the parade on the playground, in a nearby classroom, on the way to the bus, or as part of a visit to a senior citizens center.

9. Invite a doctor or nurse to class. Ask her to wear her scrub uniform complete with hat. Ask her to explain why she needs to wear the hat.

10. Visit a high school football or baseball practice session. Ask the children to inspect the special protective hats that players wear.

11. Invite a drum major or someone from a marching band to wear her uniform, complete with hat, to class to show the children.

12. Invite someone from a fife and drum corps to visit the school and show the children the colonial three-corner hat that he wears.

PHYSICAL DEVELOPMENT

1. Put a row of hats on the floor and challenge the children to jump over the hats. To make this activity more challenging, you can use larger hats or more than one row of hats.

2. Place a hat upside down on the floor. Give the children index cards and invite them to try to toss the cards into the crown of the hat.

3. Create a game similar to horseshoe toss. Invite the children to try to toss a large hat onto a weighted-down gallon jug or other suitable target.

4. Put on some music and invite the children to do their own version of the Mexican Hat Dance.

5. Have a collection of hats that use snaps, buttons, Velcro, or buckles to secure a brim or close under the chin. Invite the children to experiment with the different ways we can secure a hat.

6. Invite the children to run from Point A to Point B while wearing different hats. Be sure to include large-brim lightweight sunhats as well as baseball caps and berets. Ask the children which hats they liked to wear the most when running.

7. Invite the children to put on a hat and then try to balance a small book or other object on their head as they move from Point A to Point B.

CREATIVITY

1. Discuss with the children the idea of a magic hat. Ask the children what they would want a magic hat to do, or what magic powers they would want it to give them.

2. Present a problem for two children to solve by working together.
Place a baseball cap on a child's head and ask her to sit on the floor or in a chair. Pick another child to be the helper. Ask the two children to work together to try and remove the baseball cap without using their hands. To make this activity more challenging, you could ask the children to move the hat to Point A once it has been removed from the child's head. You could also use a ski hat instead of a baseball cap.

3. Ask the children to invent a dance that makes use of hats.

4. In Korea, they perform a traditional dance called the ribbon hat dance. Wearing pointed hats with several long ribbons attached to the top, the dancers move their heads to get the ribbons to twirl and move in very special ways. Make simple paper hats with long ribbons. Invite the children to put on the hats and make the ribbons twirl by moving their heads while they dance.

5. Organize a silly hat party. Invite the children to make and decorate silly paper hats.

6. Encourage the children to create crowns and then pretend to be kings and queens.

7. Ask the children to design a new special hat, and discuss the color, shape, and special things their hat would have.

8. Put hats out on the playground for the children to enjoy.

7

Index Cards

At any office supply store, you will find a large variety of inexpensive index cards. They come in different sizes, and can be lined, unlined, or have a grid pattern. They also come in many colors ranging from blue, yellow, and purple, to orange, bright pink, and lime green. This wonderful variety can be put to good use.

HELP CHILDREN DISCOVER

1. People use index cards to write on.

2. Index cards can be used in many different ways—for example, to store recipes, addresses, or other information.

3. Index cards come in different sizes.

4. Index cards come in different colors.

5. Index cards can be lined, unlined, or have a grid pattern.

6. Index cards are usually kept in small file boxes.

LITERACY

1. Print all of the letters that are needed to make the children's names on 3" × 5" index cards. Print one letter of the alphabet on each card. For example, Ellen requires one uppercase E, two lowercase l, one lowercase e, and one lower-case n. Scatter the cards on a table. Challenge the children to find the letters they need to make their name. This activity can be made simpler by limiting the number of letters and children participating at any one time. For example, you could start with the letters for the names of just one or two children. This activity can be made more challenging by asking the children to find the letters of a friend's name. If this is too challenging, write their friend's name down on a slip of paper.

2. Invite the children to play a letter-matching game. Cut 4" × 6" index cards in half. Print a letter of the alphabet on each half of a cut index card. Be sure to make at least two cards for each letter. Hand out one card to each child. Tell the children you are going to play some music for them to dance or march to and that when the

music stops they should find and stand by the other children who have the same letter of the alphabet printed on their cards. After the children have found the classmates with the matching letters, collect the cards, shuffle and redistribute them. Repeat the activity as many times as the children would like. This activity can be made more challenging by using more letters, uppercase and lowercase letters, or by printing simple words such as "zoo," "stop," and "go" instead of letters.

3. To encourage dramatic play, set up a vision test area. Prepare an eye chart with items drawn smaller and smaller as you go lower on the chart. Ask the children to hold up an index card to cover one eye as they read the chart. To make this activity more challenging, print letters on the chart.

4. Fasten a string (approximately four to six feet in length) to a wall, so that it resembles a clothesline. Position the string at the children's eye level. Print letters of the alphabet on index cards. Print one letter of the alphabet on each index card and then use tape to attach the index cards to the string. Prepare a set of cards using the same letters and place them in a container. Ask the children to select a card from the container, then walk over to the clothesline and point to the matching letter. To make this activity simpler, use fewer letters. To make this activity more challenging, ask the children to identify the letter and say a word that starts with the same sound as the letter they identified. Another variation on this activity would be to ask the children to walk over to the letters and tap the letters that are in their name.

5. On an index card, use glue to print a letter. Invite the children to pour sand over the card to make a sand letter. To make this activity more challenging, ask the children to print a letter using the glue, and then pour sand over it.

6. Invite the children to be authors and illustrators, and create their own books. Ask the children to draw on several small pieces of paper. Then, ask the children to decorate large-size index cards to be used as book covers. Staple the pieces of paper and index cards together to make a book. Next, ask the children to dictate stories that you then write on the pages of their books. Encourage the children to read each other's books.

7. Place different-color index cards in a container. Invite the children to reach in the container and pick out a card. Then, challenge the children to find items in the room that are the same color as the index card. You could also use a crayon or marker to put different colors on white index cards.

8. Place a collection of different-color index cards on a table. Challenge the children to sort the index cards by color.

9. Create a letter-fishing game. Print letters of the alphabet on index cards. Print one letter on each card. Fasten a large metal paper clip to each index card. Place the cards on the floor with the letters clearly visible. Use a string to attach a magnet to a fishing pole. Invite the children to use the pole to go fishing for letters. To make this activity more challenging, ask the children to identify the letter that they caught and say a word that starts with the same sound as that letter.

10. Draw pictures on index cards of happy, sad, and surprised faces. Show the children the drawings on the index cards and then discuss with them what makes them happy, sad, or surprised.

11. Use index cards with letters printed on them when singing the song Bingo with the children. Print an index card for each letter of the song: B-I-N-G-O. Place the cards on a flannel board or tape them to an easel or display board. While the children are singing the song, remove or turn over the correct letter when the children clap their hands, instead of saying the letter. For example, remove the B when the children clap once and sing I-N-G-O. To make this activity more challenging, print the name of each child in your group on separate index cards. Show the children an index card and ask them to identify whose name is printed on the card. Then, sing the melody of Bingo but substitute the letters of a child's name for B-I-N-G-O. The rhythm may need to be modified, but the children will be delighted to sing songs using their names.

12. Use index cards to create a concentration game. Cut a 4" × 6" or a 5" × 8" index card in half. On one half of the card, draw a dot, line, or geometric shape using a marker. Using the same marker, draw the same illustration on the other half of the card. To start, make three sets of cards using different colors for each set. Place the cards on the floor, illustration side down. Ask the children to turn the cards over to find the matching pairs. This activity can be made more challenging by using more pairs of cards. You can also make cards that use letters of the alphabet or simple pictures of animals or items. Whenever possible, print the name of the color or item under the illustration. For those children who are ready, you could print the names of the children in the class, or simple words such as "stop," "exit," or "go" instead of drawing illustrations on the index cards.

13. Use index cards to make signs to tape to the structures that the children have built in the block corner. Ask the children if they would like signs, such as "Hospital," "Airport," "Hotel," or "School." Encourage the children to think of their own ideas for signs that they would like to have made. To make this activity more challenging, encourage the children to print their own signs.

14. Create a beanbag toss game. Print some of the letters of the alphabet on large-size index cards. Print one letter on each card. Place the index cards close together on the floor. Tape the cards to the floor so they do not slide or move around. Invite a child to stand with her back to the letters. Then, ask the child to toss a beanbag over her shoulder in the direction of the letters. Ask the child to turn around and identify the letter the beanbag landed on. To make this activity more challenging, ask the child to say a word that starts with the same sound as the letter the beanbag landed on.

MATHEMATICS

1. Cut index cards to match the size of the squares on a page from an old calendar. Write numbers on the squares to correspond to the number of days in a month. Invite the children to match the numbered index card squares to the correct squares on the calendar. To make this activity simpler, use fewer numbers.

2. Draw a line on a large-size index card. Ask the children to estimate how many tokens will fit on the line. Ask the children to place tokens on the line and then count them. This activity can be made more challenging by lengthening the size of the line drawn or by asking the children to use increasingly smaller tokens to cover the line.

3. Draw simple geometric shapes on individual index cards—for example, a circle or a triangle. Show the children an index card and challenge them to use their fingers, hands, arms, or bodies to match the figures on the cards.

4. Create a game. Cut 4" × 6" index cards in half. On one half of a card, write the number 1. On the other half of the card, draw one dot. Do the same with the correct corresponding number of dots for the numbers 2, 3, 4, and 5. Shuffle the index cards and place them face side up on a table. Invite the children to match the card with the number to the card with the corresponding number of dots. This activity can be made more challenging by using higher numbers and including a card for zero. You could enrich this activity by printing the words for the numbers under the numbers.

> You could enrich this activity by printing the words for the numbers under the numbers.

5. Roll a large index card to form a tube. Secure with a piece of tape. Challenge the children to find items that will fit in the tube or easily go through the tube.

6. Place a collection of various sizes of index cards on a table. Invite the children to sort the cards by size. Talk about length and width with the children.

7. Create a puzzle. Draw a geometric shape such as a triangle or circle on a large index card. Then, cut the card into two or three pieces. Invite the children to put the pieces together to form the geometric shape. This activity can be made more challenging by increasing the number of puzzle pieces per geometric shape or by using the pieces for two or three different geometric shapes at the same time.

8. Place an assortment of index cards on a table. Invite the children to measure the index cards.

9. Invite the children to cut an index card in half, thirds, or quarters. Challenge the children to cut an index card on a diagonal to create two triangles.

10. On index cards, write the numbers 0 to 5. Write one number on each index card. Invite the children to put the cards in the correct order from the lowest to the highest number. To make this activity more challenging, use more numbers.

11. Use index cards to create a simplified version of the card game War, where each child turns over a card and the child with the highest number gets to keep the other cards. Write the numbers 1 to 5 on index cards. Write one number on each card. You could also include a card with a symbol such as a star or smiley face, which would be a winner-take-all card. Make several sets of the cards. Shuffle the cards, and give each child a stack of cards number side down. Start the game by asking each child to turn over a card. This activity can be made

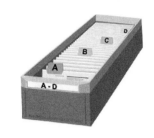

more challenging by using higher numbers and including zero. To make this activity simpler, draw the corresponding number of dots under the numbers you write on the cards.

12. Cut index cards into geometric figures such as circles, squares, rectangles, and triangles. Invite the children to sort the cards by shape.

13. Invite a child to tap out a rhythm on a tabletop using an index card—for example, tap, tap, pause, tap. Then, ask the other children to match that rhythm.

SCIENCE

1. Roll large index cards to form megaphones. Use tape to secure the cone-shaped cards. Invite the children to experiment with the megaphones. Encourage the children to place their megaphone next to their mouth and listen carefully as they sing or say something into the megaphone.

2. Tape different items to index cards, such as nails, bottle caps, aluminum foil, ribbons, paper clips, or flower petals. Place the index cards with the items facing down on the floor. Challenge the children to slowly move a magnet over the cards and find the cards that are attracted to the magnet.

3. Create a visual perception activity. In the center of an index card, draw a circle using three or four dashes instead of a solid line. Ask the children to take a close look at the drawing. Through the center of this circle, push the pointed end of a pencil. The card should be positioned about one inch above the point of the pencil. Invite the children to spin the pencil like a top. Some children might find it easier to roll the pencil back and forth between the palms of their hands while looking at the index card. Encourage the children to observe the drawing on the index card. If rotated quickly enough, the dotted lines will appear to be connected. You can also

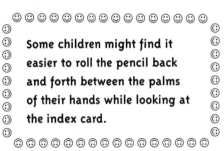

Some children might find it easier to roll the pencil back and forth between the palms of their hands while looking at the index card.

ask the children to create another optical illusion. On an index card, draw a fish. On another index card that is the same size, draw a fish bowl. Staple the cards together back to back, with the illustrations clearly visible. Then, place a dowel in between the cards and fasten securely. Ask the children to place the dowel in the palm of their hands and move it back and forth, so the index cards spin freely. The movement of the cards will create the optical illusion of the fish being in the bowl.

4. Invite the children to tap a single index card on a table or a hollow block and listen carefully to the sound. Then, ask the children to listen for any differences in the sound when they tap a stack of 5, 10, 30, or more index cards on the table or the block.

5. Place several index cards in different pans of water. Encourage the children to observe the cards and water after several hours or the next day. Be sure to use index cards of different sizes and colors.

6. Place small items such as a blade of grass, strand of hair, flower petal, or string on white unlined index cards. Place only one item on each index card. Secure the item by taping one end of the item to the index card. Invite the children to use a magnifying glass to examine these items.

7. Place containers, sand, and several index cards in the sensory table for the children to experiment with. Fold some index cards in half. Roll some index cards into the shape of a funnel and secure with tape. The children may use the index cards as scoops or funnels to channel sand into small containers.

8. Cut a square or rectangle out of the middle of a large index card. Tape a piece of colored cellophane over the cutout geometric shape. Invite the children to look through the cellophane. You could also tape other materials over the cutout geometric shape for the children to look through, such as colored tissue paper, thin cotton, or silk. To make this activity even more interesting, include materials that are not transparent, such as construction paper or aluminum foil. This activity provides an opportunity to introduce the words "opaque," "transparent," and "translucent."

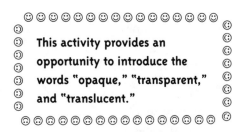

This activity provides an opportunity to introduce the words "opaque," "transparent," and "translucent."

9. On a 5" × 8" index card, draw a large distinct pattern, such as an X or two parallel lines. Invite the children to use a hole-punch or a pencil to make several holes on the pattern. Tape the index card to a windowpane that gets direct sunlight. Encourage the children to observe how the beams of sunlight that pass through the holes of the card move from one location to another during the course of the day. When the beams fall on the floor or a wall, they will match the pattern of holes that were made on the card.

10. Ask the children to examine, fold, crumple, or tear dry index cards. Then, ask the children to do the same to index cards that have been submerged in water for a few minutes or for a longer time, such as an hour or a day. Discuss with the children the differences in the cards. Invite the children to speculate about what would happen to the cards if they were placed in a freezer for a few hours. Then, place the dry cards in one Ziploc bag and the wet cards in another Ziploc bag, and put the cards in the freezer. Remove the index cards from the freezer after an hour or two. Encourage the children to examine the wet and dry index cards and discuss how the index cards feel, and what (if anything) happened as a result of putting the index cards in the freezer.

11. Invite the children to make shadows using large index cards. Place index cards on a table and invite the children to cut the cards into simple geometric shapes or to use a hole-punch to make holes in the index cards. Show the children how to make shadows with their cards by holding an index card by one corner and then standing between a source of light and a sheet, or a source of light and a wall. Encourage the children to experiment and move their index cards first toward and then away from the source of light and observe what happens to the size of the shadows.

SOCIAL STUDIES

1. Ask each child to bring in a small photo of someone from their home. Use index cards to create frames for the photos and then put them on a bulletin board in the room.

2. Invite someone who works in an office to come to class and explain how he uses index cards.

3. Ask the children to use small index cards as invitation cards. Ask the children to help make invitations for the children next door to join your class for lunch or some other special activity.

4. Visit an office supply store to see all the different kinds of index cards.

5. Visit a library or supermarket and check the community bulletin board. Look for index cards with information about job opportunities, things for sale, or upcoming events.

6. Create an appreciation bulletin board. On index cards, write down what children say about a person that helps them at school, such as a bus driver or the person that helps keep the school clean. Post the index cards on a bulletin board in a hallway for all to see.

7. Ask families to send in recipes printed on index cards of a favorite family dish. Try to prepare the dish at school, or if possible plan a special event where families bring in a favorite dish to share. Print the name and recipe for the dish on index cards and place them next to the dish.

PHYSICAL DEVELOPMENT

1. Invite the children to fold, bend, tear, or cut index cards.

2. Play a game where the children pick an index card and then have to do what is printed on the card, such as "run," jump," "slide," or "walk backward."

3. Invite the children to use a hole-punch to make designs on index cards.

4. Challenge the children to walk from Point A to Point B with an index card balanced on one hand. To make this activity more challenging, ask the children to balance the card on their head, or to slide, or to walk backward while balancing the index card.

5. Create a pattern on an index card using a hole-punch and invite the children to use yarn, string, or a shoelace to sew the pattern.

6. Challenge the children to fold an index card to create a fan.

7. Invite the children to toss index cards into a hat or laundry basket.

8. Cut colored index cards into small squares or circles. Ask the children to use a hole-punch to make a hole in the center of each piece. Invite the children to thread a piece of yarn or string through the holes and create a necklace.

9. Scatter a collection of the same size index cards on a table. Challenge the children to put the index cards together to form a neat stack.

CREATIVITY

1. Challenge the children to come up with different uses for index cards.

2. Add some index cards to the block corner.

3. Put some index cards in the sandbox or out on the playground.

4. Invite the children to create a tile or mosaic design collage by using small square pieces that have been cut from different-colored index cards.

5. To encourage dramatic play, set up an office. Be sure to include index cards in the office supplies.

6. Show the children an assortment of different-colored index cards and challenge them to invent a new game using the index cards.

7. Encourage the children to talk about creating new recipes for dishes they would like to eat. Write the recipes down on index cards.

8
Mail

Many teachers talk about mail as a part of their Valentine's Day activities. I think mail is a rich topic and deserves time and attention above and beyond Valentine's Day. For a young child, getting mail is a special event. You can purchase inexpensive stamps ranging in price from one to five cents. As an added bonus, when you explore mail with the children you will actually find some use for your junk mail! Be sure you do not give the children any mail containing confidential information.

HELP CHILDREN DISCOVER

1. Mail is a form of communication.

2. Different things come in the mail—for example, bills, letters, birthday cards, postcards, magazines, advertisements, mail order catalogs, and packages.

3. We purchase stamps and put them on letters and packages to pay for the cost of delivering the mail.

4. There are different ways to send mail, such as priority or express mail.

5. We can buy stamps and mail letters or packages at the post office.

6. Mail carriers deliver mail. They put mail in mailboxes.

7. Stationery with your name and address can be made just for you. Stationery comes in many different colors and typefaces.

LITERACY

1. Invite the children to help you compose and decorate a letter written on stationery in order to develop a pen pal correspondence. A pen pal does not have to be someone hundreds of miles away. It could be someone in a senior citizens center 10 miles away, in a nearby school, or in a class next door.

2. Ask parents to send in two envelopes each with their return address in the upper-left-hand corner. Request

> A pen pal does not have to be someone hundreds of miles away. It could be someone in a senior citizens center 10 miles away, in a nearby school, or in a class next door.

that they use identical address stickers or stamps if they have them, or just carefully print their name and address in the proper location. Show the children the envelopes and discuss the different types of return address labels with the children. For example, some may have illustrations, be printed in different colors, or use raised letters. Put the envelopes on a table and invite the children to find envelopes with matching return addresses. This activity can be made simpler by limiting the number of envelopes to be matched to three or four pairs.

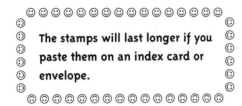

The stamps will last longer if you paste them on an index card or envelope.

3. Place a collection of stamps on a table and ask the children to sort them. Stamps can be purchased for as little as one to five cents. The stamps will last longer if you paste them on an index card or envelope.

4. Randomly print a few letters on a piece of paper. Invite the children to paste one-cent stamps on the letters. To make this activity more challenging, print more letters, and talk about the letters as the children paste the stamps on them.

5. Give the children mail order catalogs. Challenge the children to look for pictures of items that are red, then cut or tear the pictures out and place them in an envelope that has a red mark on it, or the word red printed on it. This activity can be made more challenging by asking the children to look for more than one color, or to look for items that begin with the sound of the letter B, or items that rhyme with a particular word—for example, mat or hat. Be careful not to ask the children to do more than they are ready to do. This activity should be interesting and fun, not frustrating.

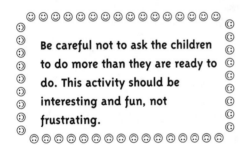

Be careful not to ask the children to do more than they are ready to do. This activity should be interesting and fun, not frustrating.

6. Challenge the children to find specific letters printed on an envelope as part of an address or return address. To make this activity more challenging, ask the children to look for the letters in their names on the envelope. You could also ask the children to look for combinations of letters—for example, "Mr.," "Ave.," or "St." To make this activity simpler, print letters on index cards and ask the children to find the matching letters on the envelope.

7. Encourage the children to look for promotional postcards in magazines.

8. With the children, look through mail order catalogs or brochures for educational toys or books. Discuss the different items that can be ordered, and then select a book or toy to order. Place the order and wait for the package to be delivered by the mail carrier.

9. Place an assortment of scraps of colored paper on a table. Invite the children to pick a piece of colored paper and then look for that color in advertisements from junk mail.

10. Set up mailboxes for everyone in the room. Print the children's names on their mailboxes. Prepare envelopes with the children's names on them and ask someone to be a delivery person. To make this activity simpler, you can use shapes, colors, patterns, or numbers in addition to the children's names to help

identify the children's mailboxes. To encourage letter writing, set up a letter-writing center with paper, envelopes, crayons, and pencils. Invite the children to write letters and deliver them to their friends' mailboxes.

11. Show the children some picture postcards. Ask the children to talk about postcards that they have received from grandparents, family, or friends.

12. Set up a post office to encourage dramatic play.

13. Invite the children to mail a letter or piece of artwork to someone in their family. Ask the children to help address the envelope or to watch you do it.

14. With the children, write and mail a thank-you note to someone who has visited the class and given a demonstration.

15. Surprise the children by writing and mailing a short letter to each child in your class. The children will enjoy the experience of receiving a letter addressed to them.

MATHEMATICS

1. Create a number-matching game. Draw a mailbox for each child on a piece of paper. In the middle of each mailbox, write a street address number—for example, 9311. On a table, place an assortment of stick-on numbers for mailboxes. (These numbers can be purchased at a home improvement center, or you can make your own using black construction paper.) Challenge the children to find the correct numbers for their mailbox. This activity can be made simpler by printing only one or two numbers on the mailboxes. To make this activity more challenging, give each child a blank mailbox. Then, prepare a set of index cards with one to five dots on each card. Invite the children to pick a card, count the dots, and then select the corresponding number sticker for their mailbox.

2. Place an assortment of different-size greeting cards and their matching envelopes on a table. Challenge the children to find the envelope that is the correct size for each greeting card.

3. Purchase several stamps of different face values. Paste individual stamps on index cards and then invite the children to order the stamps from the least to the most expensive. To make this activity more challenging, you could use more stamps of higher value. If the children are developmentally ready, you could paste more than one stamp on a card. For example, paste a one-cent stamp and a two-cent stamp on an index card, or paste two one-cent stamps on an index card.

4. Create a game using a die with one, two, and three dots on it. Draw four equal sections on a piece of construction paper. Place a collection of stamps worth from one to three cents on the table. Ask the children to roll the die, identify the number, and then pick the stamp with the corresponding value as the number of dots on the die, and place it in a section on the paper. The game is over when the child has four stamps on the paper.

5. Create a shape-matching activity. Draw geometric shapes on envelopes. Draw one shape per envelope. You could use a business envelope or a large manila envelope. Place several pieces of paper that have been cut into different geometric shapes on a table. Challenge the children to put the geometric shapes into the envelopes that have the same geometric shapes drawn on them. To make this activity more challenging, you could ask the children to count how many pieces of paper (rectangles, triangles, or circles) they put in each envelope.

6. Create a number-matching game. Place some envelopes on a table. On an index card, write a number and then ask the children to look for that number in the street addresses or zip codes printed on the envelopes. To make this activity more challenging, ask the children to look for higher or two-digit numbers, such as "12."

7. Ask the children to estimate how many large manila envelopes, when placed end to end on the floor, are needed to go from Point A to Point B. With the children, put the envelopes on the floor and then count them. To make this activity more challenging, use smaller envelopes.

8. Place an assortment of envelopes on a table. Invite the children to order the envelopes by size from the smallest to the largest. To make this activity more challenging, ask the children to measure the sizes of the envelopes.

9. Give the children an assortment of papers. Challenge the children to pick a piece of paper and fold it so it will fit in an envelope. It may need to be folded in half or in thirds.

10. With the help of the children fill several priority or express mailboxes with different items and seal the boxes. Then, challenge the children to order the boxes from the lightest to the heaviest. You could also ask the children to weigh the boxes.

11. Encourage the children to estimate how many blocks will fit in a priority or express mailbox. With the children, count the blocks as they fill the box. To make this activity more challenging, repeat this activity using smaller blocks or a larger box.

12. Encourage the children to look through a mail order catalog. Ask the children to find and count the number of things that they would like to order. Limit the search to one page. You could also ask the children to count items that are small, large, used outdoors, or any other classification you wish to use. To make this activity more challenging, ask the children to look on more than one page, or look for a specific number of items, such as five or 10 hats.

13. Invite the children to go on a treasure hunt. Place index cards with numbers written on them in a large manila envelope. Ask a child to reach in the envelope, pull out an index card and identify the number written on it. Give each child a letter size or manila envelope and challenge the children to find the same number of items as the number identified, and place them in the envelope. This activity can be made more challenging if you use higher numbers or

smaller-size envelopes. Spatial judgment will become a factor as the children try to fit the correct number of items into the envelope.

SCIENCE

1. Place a collection of mail on a table. Invite the children to sort the different things that come in the mail. For example, greeting cards, postcards, advertisements, or magazines.

2. Out of the sight of the children, put different items in several envelopes and seal them. Be sure to put metal items in some of the envelopes. Invite the children to use a magnet to find out which envelopes contain items that are attracted to the magnet.

3. Place a collection of picture postcards on a table and invite the children to sort them. The postcards can be sorted in many different ways—for example, by color, or by type such as scenery, animals, or paintings from art museums.

4. Out of the sight of the children, put different items in sealed envelopes. Place the sealed envelopes on a table. Invite the children to use their sense of touch to try to identify what is inside the envelopes. Encourage the children to describe the items using words like hard, small, and round.

5. Set up a table with a magnifying glass and several types of stationery. Invite the children to observe the different papers used to make stationery. You should also have several postage stamps available for the children to inspect.

6. Create a touch table. On the table, place cards and stationery with engraving or raised printing on them. Invite the children to feel the raised print.

7. Place a collection of different envelopes on a table. Include different colors and sizes, and some with and without windows. Invite the children to sort the envelopes by color, size, or any criteria they select.

8. Out of the sight of the children, place different items in envelopes such as coins, sand, leaves, or flower petals. Put only one type of item in each envelope. Seal the envelopes. Place the same items on a table. Invite the children to shake the envelopes and listen to the different sounds that are made. Then, ask the children to select from the table the item that they think is in each envelope.

9. Put some water in the sensory table. Give the children different envelopes, including some that are padded and lined with plastic. Encourage the children to experiment with the envelopes and observe what happens when they become wet.

10. Discuss with the children things that might not be able to be sent in the mail such as animals or plants. Talk about the reasons why they cannot be put in the mail.

11. Experiment with a megaphone. Give a child a mailing tube and encourage him to listen carefully as he makes sounds or talks into the tube.

SOCIAL STUDIES

1. Ask family members to bring a letter to class from a friend or relative in another town or country and read part of the letter to the children.

2. Ask family members to bring in some stamps from other countries and invite the children to examine them.

3. Go outside and look for the address number of your school, then take a walk and look for address numbers on houses or buildings in the neighborhood. Also, look for the nearest mailbox.

4. Visit a home improvement center and look at the different mailboxes that are for sale. You could also walk or drive through a community where mailboxes are located at curbside and notice the different styles of mailboxes.

5. Ask the children to cooperate and see how many empty priority or express mailboxes they can stack on top of one another.

6. With the children, compose, address and mail an invitation to each of the children and their families inviting them to come to class for a special event. The event can be as simple as a special snack time.

7. Visit a post office and ask to see mail delivery trucks.

8. Try to arrange for the children to meet the mail carrier that brings mail to your center and follow the distribution process.

9. Visit a stationery store. They may have some extra books of samples of different types of stationery or printing that they may be willing to give you.

10. Try to arrange to visit a large apartment complex and watch the mail carrier deliver the mail.

11. Look for a mail chute in a large office building.

12. Encourage the children to create works of art to give to people to cheer them up. Mail the works of art to someone in a hospital or at a senior citizens center.

PHYSICAL DEVELOPMENT

1. Invite the children to open junk mail envelopes.

2. Encourage the children to use tricycles as mail trucks on the playground. Provide some props such as mailbags, mailboxes, and letters to be delivered.

3. Tape some envelopes to the floor and invite the children to jump or crawl from one envelope to another. This activity can be made more challenging if you print letters or numbers on the envelopes and then invite the children to jump or crawl to a specific letter or number, or go to envelopes in a specific order such as A, B, C or 1, 2, 3.

4. Challenge the children to fold a piece of paper with letters or simple words printed on it, and place the paper into a window envelope with the letters or words showing correctly through the window.

5. Challenge the children to carry a stack of empty priority or express mailboxes from Point A to Point B. The children can also run, slide, or walk backward while carrying the boxes.

6. Invite several children to see how many of their hands they can fit in a priority or express mailbox at the same time. Then, challenge the children to walk from Point A to Point B while keeping their hands in the box.

7. Challenge the children to roll a piece of paper so that it will fit in a mailing tube.

8. Challenge the children to move a mailing tube, or a priority or express mail box from Point A to Point B without using their hands.

CREATIVITY

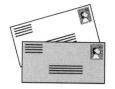

1. Invite the children to handle and inspect a padded mailing envelope. Discuss with the children what they might put in the envelope to be mailed.

2. Invite the children to look at a picture of a person in an advertisement that came in the mail. Ask the children to suggest names for that person.

3. Ask the children for ideas about how to use envelopes for things other than letters—for example, to hold seeds, paper clips, or recipe cards.

4. Show the children a picture of a smiling person in a mail order catalog. Ask the children, "Why do you think this person is smiling?" or "Why do you think this person is happy?" Before asking the children for their ideas, offer suggestions—for example, "It's her birthday," "Grandma is coming to visit," or "She is going to have pizza for dinner."

> Before asking the children for their ideas, offer suggestions—for example, "It's her birthday," "Grandma is coming to visit," or "She is going to have pizza for dinner."

5. Invite the children to create a collage using colorful scraps of paper from junk mail.

6. Ask the children if they would like to write a letter to a famous person—for example, a sports star, singer, or astronaut. Discuss with the children what they would like to write.

7. Discuss with the children some things that could be mailed in an express mailbox.

8. Invite the children to place different items in mailing tubes, seal the tubes, and then listen to the sounds that are made when they shake the mailing tubes. Play some music and invite the children to be part of a rhythm band.

9

Mittens and Gloves

At last, something you can do with all those lost and mismatched mittens and gloves that are left at school each year! Mittens and gloves can be very important items. In addition to keeping hands warm, specially designed gloves and mittens are used to protect hands from dirt, heat, water, splinters, electric current, or fire. Butchers use specially made metal gloves to protect their hands when using large knives to cut meat. Dentists, nurses, and doctors use gloves to protect against the spread of bacteria and disease. Gloves are also important in sports: golfers, baseball players, hockey players, rock climbers, skiers, and football players all wear specially designed gloves.

HELP CHILDREN DISCOVER

1. Gloves and mittens come in different sizes.

2. Gloves and mittens are made from many different materials.

3. Some gloves and mittens keep our hands warm.

4. Specially designed gloves and mittens protect our hands from being hurt.

5. Some gloves keep our hands dry.

6. Some gloves are part of a uniform, such as for a police officer or firefighter.

7. Some gloves are designed to be worn when participating in sports.

LITERACY

1. Put several pairs of mittens on a table and invite the children to match the mittens to form pairs.

2. Tape to the palm side of a mitten a piece of paper with a letter printed on it. The top of the letter should be by the fingers. Be sure you prepare at least two mittens with the same letter for each letter you print. Ask the children to stand in a circle. Give one mitten to each child. Ask the children to put the mitten on

and then hold up the hand with the mitten on it. Challenge the children to walk around and find the other children who are wearing a mitten with the matching letter. This activity can be made more challenging by asking the children to identify the letter and say a word that begins with that letter. Another variation on this activity would be to ask the children to create nonsense words that begin with the same sound as the letter. For example, for the letter b a child could say "beeglo" or "baak." This activity can also be made more challenging by using more children and more letters, using uppercase and lowercase letters, or simple words for the children to match.

3. Organize a treasure hunt. Show the children a mitten that is a solid color—for example, red. Ask the children to locate items in the room that are the same color as the mitten. To make this activity more challenging, show the children a mitten with two or three colors. Challenge the children to find an item for each of the colors of the mitten.

4. Create a concentration game using pairs of mittens. Place a mitten under a small box. Place the matching mitten from the pair under another small box. Do this for three or four pairs of mittens. Invite the children to play concentration and look under the boxes for matching pairs of mittens. You can use pairs of gloves instead of mittens or pairs of gloves and mittens.

5. Place an assortment of gloves on a table. Challenge the children to match the gloves to a picture of the person that uses that glove. For example, the children could match a garden glove with a gardener, a baseball glove with a baseball player.

6. Create a recipe chart, and invite the children to follow the directions and help make some muffins. Be sure the children see you use an oven mitt to remove the muffins from the oven.

7. Invite the children to look for specific letters printed on baseball gloves or hockey gloves.

8. Place an assortment of gloves and mittens on a table for the children to examine. Then, discuss with the children how the gloves and mittens are alike and how they are different.

9. Create a letter-matching game. Print letters of the alphabet on small pieces of paper and place them in a large mitten. On a piece of construction paper, print the name of a child. Invite that child to reach into the mitten and try to find letters that match the letters in his name. This activity can be made simpler by placing just a few letters in the mitten. It can be made more challenging by using more letters or simple words such as "look," "stop," "red, "blue," or "mommy" instead of printing the children's names.

10. Use a story glove when doing a finger play, such as "Five Little Monkeys Jumping on the Bed." Challenge the children to create a new story using the story glove.

11. Invite the children to examine a variety of gloves such as heavy-duty work gloves, dishwashing gloves, disposable gloves, scuba diving gloves, firefighter's

gloves, and a butcher's protective glove. Discuss with the children how the gloves help protect hands.

12. To encourage dramatic play, put different types of gloves in the dramatic play area. Be sure to include elbow-length gloves for formal occasions.

MATHEMATICS

1. Invite the children to count the fingers on a glove or a pair of gloves.

2. Tape to the palm side of a mitten a piece of paper with a number written on it. Be sure to include zero. The top of the number should be by the fingers. Prepare two or more mittens for each number you use. Ask the children to stand in a circle. Hand out one mitten to each child. Ask the children to put the mitten on and hold up the hand with the mitten on it. Challenge the children to walk around to find the other children who are wearing a mitten with the same number. This activity can be made more challenging by using more children and higher numbers. You could also prepare one mitten with a number and one mitten with the corresponding number of dots and challenge the children to find the mittens that belong together. Instead of numbers and dots, you could prepare mittens with only dots for the children to match. Another variation would be to ask the children to line up from the lowest (smallest) to highest (largest) number—for example, 0 to 5.

3. Prepare mittens as in the activity above, but this time use geometric shapes, such as circles, rectangles, and triangles, instead of numbers for the children to match.

4. Challenge the children to order by length a collection of gloves and mittens. Be sure to include mittens for infants, children, and adults.

5. Invite the children to measure the length of the different fingers of a child's glove. Ask the children to identify the shortest and longest finger. To make this activity more challenging, add an adult's glove and ask the children to compare the two.

6. Invite the children to estimate how many small items such as wood pegs will fit in a mitten. Then, with the children, count the items as they are put in the mitten. For comparison, you could also ask the children to estimate how many items will fit in a similar-size glove.

7. Create a game using a spinner. Place a bowl of tokens on a table. Give each child a similar-size mitten. When the child spins a number, have her identify the number and put that number of tokens in her mitten. When the mitten is full, the game is over. To make this activity more challenging, ask each child to count how many tokens it took to fill up their mitten. You could also use a die or a pair of dice instead of a spinner. To make this activity simpler, use larger-size tokens.

8. Encourage the children to look inside a glove for the label indicating size.

9. Create a graph of the colors found in the children's mittens.

10. Create a treasure hunt game. Ask each child to find two items that will fit into a mitten at the same time—for example, two small toy cars. To make this activity more challenging, ask the children to find three, four, or eight items that will fit in a mitten. This will challenge the children's spatial thinking. As the number of items increase, they will have to find smaller and smaller objects.

11. Fill several mittens with different items such as nails, rocks, and paper scraps. Close the top of each mitten with a rubber band. Challenge the children to order the mittens by weight, from the lightest to the heaviest.

SCIENCE

1. Put water in the sensory table. Invite the children to use waterproof gloves and experiment (play) with the water.

2. Invite the children to clap their hands when wearing gloves or mittens made of different materials. Encourage the children to listen carefully to the different sounds each pair of gloves or mittens makes.

3. Challenge the children to pick up small items such as string, crayons, or pegs while wearing gloves or mittens made of different materials. Try to have latex, plastic, leather, fur, or wool gloves or mittens for the children to use. Discuss the thickness and flexibility of the different gloves and mittens with the children.

4. Ask the children to help you fill a rubber glove with water, close the top with a rubber band, and put it in the freezer for a few hours. Try to do the same thing with a wool mitten. Discuss with the children what happens. (The wool mitten will not hold water the way a rubber glove does so I suggest you hold it over a bowl.) After a few hours, remove the rubber glove from the freezer and encourage the children to examine the glove. Discuss their observations.

5. Create a touch game. Place an assortment of gloves on a table. Out of the sight of the children, put a glove in a bag. Invite the children to reach in the bag, touch the glove, and then try to select a glove on the table that feels the same. Be sure the assortment on the table has a glove made of the same material as the glove in the bag. Try to provide gloves that are made of different materials such as cotton, leather, wool, rubber, and gloves lined with fur for the children to touch.

6. Out of the sight of the children, drop nails and other items such as paper, wood pegs, or pebbles into different mittens. Close the tops of the mittens with rubber bands. Place the mittens on the table and challenge the children to use a magnet to locate which mitten contains the nails.

7. Place an assortment of mittens and gloves on a table. Invite the children to use a magnifying glass to closely inspect the different materials that gloves and mittens are made of. Be sure to turn a mitten and a glove inside out. Try to include baseball gloves and other gloves that are used in sports for the children to examine.

8. Place gloves or mittens made of different materials such as leather, wool, and rubber on a table. Invite the children to smell the gloves. Put a small amount of water on the gloves and mittens and then ask the children to smell the gloves again. Encourage the children to talk about how the gloves smell when dampened with water.

9. Ask each child to wear a mitten on one hand and sit in a circle. Give one child an ice cube and ask the child to hold the ice cube with both hands before passing it on to the next child in the circle. Discuss with the children the effect the mitten had on what they felt. You could also place some ice cubes and water in the sensory table. Invite the children to put their hands in the water when wearing gloves made of different materials, such as cotton or wool. Then, ask the children to put their hands in the water for a short period of time without wearing gloves. Discuss with the children the effect the gloves had on what they felt with their hands. Try to include waterproof gloves and neoprene scuba diving gloves for the children to use.

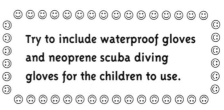

Try to include waterproof gloves and neoprene scuba diving gloves for the children to use.

10. Firefighters and some joggers use gloves with reflective tape on them. Try to bring a pair of these gloves to class, and in a dimly lit area of the room ask the children to shine a light on the reflective tape. Discuss with the children why it is important for some gloves to have reflective tape.

11. Invite the children to finger paint while wearing a plastic glove on one hand. Encourage the children to talk about how each hand feels.

12. Invite the children to start a garden. Provide garden gloves for the children to use.

SOCIAL STUDIES

1. Ask family members to bring or send to school any special gloves they have at home. Suggest that the gloves could be part of a uniform, ones that they use at work or at play, or mittens that someone in their family knitted for them. Discuss the different gloves with the children.

2. Visit the kitchen at school and observe people using plastic gloves when they are preparing food. Discuss with the children why it is important for food handlers to use plastic gloves when preparing food.

3. Visit a high school or Little League baseball team and inspect the gloves that the players use. Ask for a demonstration of how the gloves are used.

4. Invite a dentist or nurse to class. Ask her to bring her gloves and explain why she uses them.

5. Visit a nature center and ask to see the protective gloves that people wear when handling animals, or birds like owls or hawks.

6. Invite a sanitation worker, glazier, carpenter, laboratory worker, or firefighter to class to show the gloves that he uses on the job.

7. Visit a sporting goods store, and examine all the different types of gloves.

8. Visit a high school or college chemistry lab, and look at the gloves that the students wear when working in the laboratory.

9. Visit a supermarket, and ask the butcher to cut some meat and demonstrate how she uses the metal glove to protect her hand.

PHYSICAL DEVELOPMENT

1. Challenge the children to help one another put on gloves and mittens.

2. Use a string to hang a mitten filled with paper in a doorway or on a tree branch. Encourage the children to jump up to tap the mitten.

3. Fill a plastic glove with water and challenge the children to carry it from Point A to Point B without spilling any water. Provide a pail at Point B to empty the water from the glove. To make this activity more challenging, ask the children to walk backward, slide, or jump while carrying the glove filled with water. Since wet floors can be slippery, I suggest you do this activity outdoors.

4. Challenge the children to see how far they can toss a mitten. To make this activity more interesting, fill the mittens with different soft materials such as paper or cotton balls.

5. Invite the children to wear baseball gloves and play catch.

6. Challenge the children to work with crayons or markers while wearing mittens.

7. Have available a pair of white gloves. Invite the children to wear the gloves and direct tricycle traffic on the playground.

CREATIVITY

1. Discuss with the children their ideas on how to avoid losing mittens. This is an age-old problem. Archaeologists in Iceland found a pair of mittens that had been worn by a Viking child 1,100 years ago. The mittens were attached to one another by a long piece of yarn!

2. Tape long ribbons to mittens. Play some music and invite the children to wear the mittens and make the ribbons move to the music.

3. Invite the children to examine a pair of work gloves and ask them to discuss different ways they could use the gloves.

4. Challenge the children to invent a new game using mittens.

5. Make a large mitten for the flannel board. After reading the story *The Mitten* by Alvin Tresselt, invite the children to use the flannel board mitten to create another story that involves a mitten.

6. Invite the children to recycle old or torn mittens by using them to make hand puppets and then putting on a puppet show.

10

Paint and Paintings

What could be more colorful than studying paint and paintings? We use paint on walls, ceilings, doors, and furniture, and on highways, signs, toys, cars, trains, and planes. Paint is also used to create works of art. Copies of paintings by artists such as Romare Bearden, Mary Cassatt, Vincent Van Gogh, Claude Monet, Pablo Picasso, Jackson Pollock, Pierre-Auguste Renoir, Diego Rivera, and Georges Seurat will greatly enrich this theme. Inexpensive copies of paintings by well-known artists can be found in calendars, books, and art museum gift shops. Please be sure all activities involving paints are carefully supervised. The children should use only nontoxic paints.

HELP CHILDREN DISCOVER

1. Paint comes in many different colors and hues.

2. When we mix colors of paint, we can create new colors.

3. When we add different amounts of white paint to a color, we create different hues.

4. There are different kinds of paint.

5. Different paints come in different containers such as tubes, cans, or jars.

6. Paint can be applied to different surfaces such as wood, plaster, paper, or canvas.

7. Paint can be applied to surfaces in many different ways from spray cans and rollers to sponges, pallet knives, and bare hands.

8. Paint can be used to decorate or protect wood.

9. When creating paintings, artists can use different styles such as cubism, impressionism, or pointillism.

LITERACY

1. Invite the children to go on a treasure hunt. Show the children an original or copy of a painting and then ask them to find something in the room that matches one of the colors in the painting.

2. Create a color matching game. From a paint or hardware store, collect several sample cards of various paint colors. Be sure to get two of each color card you select. If each card has more than one color on it, cut the cards into individual color squares. Place the cards or squares on a table. Invite the children to find the matching colors. This activity can be made more challenging by using more colors or different hues of the same color.

3. Make original puzzles for the children to use from inexpensive print copies of art masterworks. Glue the prints to a piece of cardboard and then cut them into several pieces to make the puzzles. The more pieces you cut the more challenging the puzzle.

4. Design a letter-recognition game. Create a game board by dividing a piece of white construction paper into four different sections. In each section, paint a design using a different color. Under each design, print the name of the color of the paint used—for example, red. Prepare a stack of index cards on which you have printed the letters of the alphabet. Print one letter on each index card. Give each child a game board. Invite a child to pick a card and match it to a corresponding letter on his board. Then, ask the child to place a token on that section of the board. When all four sections are covered with a token, the game is over. This activity can be made simpler by giving the children fewer letters of the alphabet to choose from. It can be made more challenging by dividing the board into more sections with more colors and letters, or by printing uppercase and lowercase letters or the words for the colors on both the board and the index cards.

5. Out of the sight of the children, make prints of different items by dipping them in paint and pressing them on paper. Use items like a fork, feather, leaf, or the wheels of a small toy car. When dry, place the prints and items on a table and challenge the children to identify which item made which print. This activity can be made more challenging by not showing the children the items and asking them to try to determine what was used to make the print. You could also ask the children to name other things that start with the same letter as the item used to make the print. For example, if a leaf were used to make the print, the children could name a "ladder," "ladybug," or "log" as other things that start with the same letter.

Rembrandt used the wooden end of a paintbrush to scratch through wet paint in order to create textural effects.

6. Invite the children to experiment by painting with different items such as brushes, sponges, rollers, feathers, and crumpled pieces of aluminum foil. Rembrandt used the wooden end of a paintbrush to scratch through wet paint in order to create textural effects. Discuss with the children which method of painting they prefer.

7. Place a collection of different types of paints, in their original containers, on a table. Encourage the children to handle and then discuss the different containers that paints come in—for example, tubes (oil), plastic bottles (tempera), and cans (latex). You could also ask the children to look for specific letters on the containers. All the containers need to be tightly sealed so they cannot be opened by the children.

8. Fold a piece of construction paper in half, then open it up. Encourage the children to put some paint on the fold line, and then fold the paper over and press down to spread the paint. Open the paper up and let the paint dry. When the paint is dry, discuss with the children the different colors that were used and the designs that were made. Ask the children what the designs look like, or what they remind them of. This activity is similar to looking at clouds with the children and talking about the shapes they see.

9. While the children are finger painting, encourage them to draw some letters in the paint. To make this activity more challenging, ask the children to write their names in finger paint.

10. Invite the children to help paint some signs for the playground such as "STOP," "ONE WAY," "EXIT," "CHILDREN CROSSING," "PARKING," or "SPEED LIMIT 25." Encourage the children to print and create signs of their own.

11. Invite the children to paint a large box and then encourage them to use it for dramatic play.

12. Bring in an artist's palette that has been used and ask the children to identify and talk about all the colors on the palette.

13. To encourage dramatic play, bring in some paintbrushes, rollers, wet paint signs, empty paint cans, masking tape, and drop cloths. The children can pretend to paint the housekeeping area or the walls of the classroom.

14. Read any or all of the following board books written for young children by Julie Merberg and Suzanne Bober. Each book features the paintings of a famous artist. Invite the children to try the different painting techniques illustrated in the books.

A Picnic with Monet. Monet is famous for his impressionist paintings.

Sunday with Seurat. Seurat is remembered for his technique called pointillism, which uses dots to make designs and images.

Painting with Picasso. Picasso was one of the creators of the style known as cubism.

MATHEMATICS

1. Show the children some copies of paintings by Picasso. Challenge the children to locate different geometric shapes in the paintings. Invite the children to paint like Picasso and paint some geometric shapes of their own.

2. Challenge the children to look at a painting and try to count the number of different colors in the painting.

3. Encourage the children to create cardboard or paper frames for their paintings. With the children, measure the artwork to make the frames the proper size.

4. Bring in a collection of different-size paint containers, from small containers of paint for model airplanes to pint, quart, and gallon-size cans. Ask the children to order the containers from the smallest to the largest, or the lightest to the heaviest. You could also encourage the children to look for or match numbers printed on the containers.

5. Put paint in several squeeze-style ketchup bottles. Cut different-size openings in the tips of the bottles. Invite the children to use the bottles to paint templates of geometric shapes or numbers. Ask the children to observe the different widths of the streams of paint as the paint is squeezed out of the bottles.

6. Pour different amounts of paint in four or five small clear plastic cups. Encourage the children to put the cups in order, from the one with the least to the one with the most amount of paint. To make this activity more challenging, use more cups of paint.

7. Set out some paint and Q-tips. Challenge the children to use the Q-tips to paint as many dots as they can on a line that you have drawn on a piece of paper. Then, count the dots with the children. To make this activity more challenging, draw a geometric shape on a piece of paper and ask the children to try to fill the entire shape with dots. To make this activity simpler, you could ask the children to use sponges held by a spring clothespin instead of Q-tips.

8. With the children, measure several different lengths of string. Invite the children to pick which size string they would like to use for string painting.

9. Place copies of paintings of interesting buildings or structures such as skyscrapers, bridges, the ancient pyramids of Egypt, or the Roman Coliseum near the block corner. Encourage the children to notice details and differences in the architecture of each.

10. With the children, count the different colors of paint used on the walls, windows, and cabinets of your classroom. This activity can be made more challenging by counting the colors used in the hallways, offices, and other rooms in the building. You could also ask the children to count the colors of paint used on the outside of the building.

11. With the children, create a graph of their favorite paint colors.

 SCIENCE

1. Give each child a small amount of red paint in a clear plastic cup. Invite the children to add a teaspoon of white paint to the red, stir the paint, and observe the color. Then, ask the children to add another teaspoon of white paint, stir again, and observe

what happens to the color. Encourage the children to do this several times. You could also ask the children to use other colors of paint or go in the reverse direction by starting with white paint and adding a teaspoon of red paint, and then another teaspoon of red paint.

2. At the easel, put out several shades of one color of paint, such as navy blue to baby blue, for the children to experiment and paint with.

3. Create a touch table. On a table, place items that have been painted with different types of paint—for example, oil, water color, tempera, or latex. Try to include items that have been painted with different sheens, such as flat, semi-gloss, and high gloss, and items that have not been painted. Encourage the children to touch the items and discuss how they feel. You could create your own items for the touch table by painting pieces of paper or wood with different types of paint.

4. Provide a long-term observation activity for the children. Use three similar pieces of wood. With the children watching, paint one with tempera paint, one with exterior latex paint, and leave one unpainted. Place the wood out of the reach of the children until the paint is dry. Then, put the pieces of wood outdoors in a sunny area. Encourage the children to speculate about what might happen to the pieces of wood. Leave the wood outdoors for a long period of time and encourage the children to observe the wood regularly and discuss what they see.

5. Bring in some rollers that are used to apply paint. Ask the children to touch them and then to order them from the softest to the hardest. Encourage the children to use a magnifying glass to get a closer look at the rollers.

6. Put out small cups of red and blue paint. Invite the children to use a brush or Q-tip to mix the paint on paper and observe what happens. Repeat this activity using small cups of yellow and blue, and yellow and red paint. Discuss with the children what happens when the different colors are mixed.

7. Go to a paint or hardware store and get several sample color cards of different hues for one color. You could choose, for example, several shades of purple, from dark purple to lavender. If the color cards contain more than one color per card, cut the cards into individual color squares. Invite the children to arrange the color cards from the lightest to the darkest hue.

8. Encourage the children to use a magnifying glass to look at the brush strokes of an original oil painting.

9. When the children are finger painting, sprinkle some salt or sand on the paper and then encourage the children to talk about how the texture of the paint has changed.

10. Set up an experiment with the children. Pour a small amount of paint into several plastic cups. Cover all but one of the cups with different materials such as paper, plastic wrap, fabric, and aluminum foil. Leave overnight. Encourage the children to speculate about what might happen, if anything, to the paint. The next day, ask the children to inspect the paint in the different containers. Discuss with the children any changes they notice in the paint.

11. Invite the children to look at different sample paint color cards under different lighting conditions. For example, ask the children to look at the colors under fluorescent light, near a lamp, outdoors, or in dim light conditions. Encourage the children to discuss what the colors look like in each situation.

12. Place a collection of copies of masterwork paintings on a table. Ask the children, "Which pictures go together?" Discuss and accept the children's logic. Some of the criteria the children could use to sort the paintings might be size, colors used, or subject (people, flowers, or scenery).

SOCIAL STUDIES

1. Ask the children's families to send in something to class that has paint on it. They might send in anything from a piece of wood to a toy or hand-painted dishes, drinking glasses, vases, and pins. Discuss with the children the things that were sent in and how they are used. Since some of the items may be fragile, extreme care should be used during this activity.

2. Take the children for a walk in the neighborhood and look at the different colors used to paint houses or stores. You could also look at the different colors of paint used on cars.

3. Invite an artist who paints to come to class and bring some of her equipment such as an easel, paintbrushes, or palette.

4. Visit a hardware or paint store and look at all the paint and painting equipment. Try to arrange to see some paint being mixed to order.

5. Visit an art gallery or museum to look at paintings.

6. Invite someone in to the class to demonstrate and explain the significance of henna hand painting. This is an art form that has been used for thousands of years in India and the Middle East.

7. Visit an art supply store.

8. Visit a frame shop and see all the types of frames that are made for paintings.

9. Visit an automobile paint shop.

10. Visit an artist studio or art class. Try to arrange the visit so you can see painters at work.

11. Invite a house painter or commercial painter in to show the inside of his truck with paints, brushes, and ladders.

PHYSICAL DEVELOPMENT

1. Invite the children to paint with watercolors.

2. Invite the children to paint small objects such as pieces of wood.

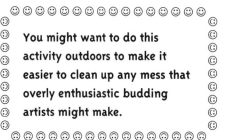

3. Paint a line on the playground, or on an old shower curtain or window shade that you securely fasten to the ground. Challenge the children to tiptoe, run, or crawl on the line. They can also jump over it.

4. Invite the children to paint a line to represent a highway on a large piece of butcher paper. When the paint is dry, challenge the children to drive small cars on the highway that they created.

5. Invite the children to use different objects or materials to apply paint—for example, Q-tips, sponges, hair rollers, cotton balls, string, feathers, or pinecones.

6. Invite the children to use rollers to paint an outside wall with water.

7. Invite the children to finger paint with their toes and feet. Ask the children to discuss how it feels.

8. Challenge the children to crawl underneath a large drop cloth that is being held close to the ground by two adults.

CREATIVITY

1. Ask the children to look at an abstract painting and discuss what they think they see in the painting.

2. Show the children a painting and invite them to make up a story about the scene, or a person or animal in the painting.

3. Show the children some copies of paintings by Jackson Pollock and discuss the creative and unusual techniques he used to apply paint to a canvas. Put a large piece of butcher paper on the floor. Give a child a paintbrush and encourage him to paint like Pollock by letting the paint drip off the paintbrush onto the paper. The child could gently move the paintbrush back and forth or in circles to help the paint drops fall off the brush. A variation on this activity would be to give the children squeeze bottles filled with paint. You might want to do this activity outdoors to make it easier to clean up any mess that overly enthusiastic budding artists might make.

> ☺☺☺☺☺☺☺☺☺☺☺☺☺☺☺
> **You might want to do this activity outdoors to make it easier to clean up any mess that overly enthusiastic budding artists might make.**
> ☺☺☺☺☺☺☺☺☺☺☺☺☺☺☺

4. Play some music near the easel while the children are painting.

5. Encourage the children to paint in different locations by moving the easel to a new location, indoors or outdoors.

6. Invite the children to paint on different planes, such as a tilted cardboard box, on the floor, or on a large piece of butcher paper taped to a wall.

7. Ask the children if they have any ideas on how they might like to paint the classroom or hallway.

8. Add variety to the easel by inviting the children to apply paint to different surfaces such as aluminum foil, corrugated cardboard, black paper, an old road map, or the want ads section of a newspaper.

11

Paper

Paper is a very rich theme because there are so many variables. It is a topic that can be explored for several weeks. Here are just a few of the possibilities that you and the children could consider. Paper comes in different sizes ranging from small note pads and legal pads to large rolls of butcher paper. There are many different weights as well, everything from tissue paper to construction paper. Newspaper, paper towels, graph paper, stationery, gift-wrap paper, sandpaper, and wallpaper are all readily available and would be interesting for the children to examine.

HELP CHILDREN DISCOVER

1. There are many different types of paper such as graph paper, stationery, construction paper, tissue paper, gift-wrap paper, wax paper, paper towels, sandpaper, and wallpaper.

2. Paper is made in different sizes, weights (thicknesses), and colors.

3. Paper is recyclable.

4. Paper can be shredded.

5. Paper is used in many different ways. For example, we use paper to make newspapers, books and bags, or to wrap things.

6. In Japan, origami (folding paper) is an art form.

7. Paper cutting is one of the oldest Chinese art forms.

LITERACY

1. Create a pattern-matching game using small pieces of wallpaper. Get a book of discontinued wallpaper samples from a home decorating store. Cut at least two pieces of wallpaper from each of several pages and place them on a table. Invite the children to match the patterns or colors. To make this activity more challenging, use more pieces of wallpaper.

2. Print a letter on a piece of paper. Ask the children to look in a newspaper for that letter to see how many they can find. The newspaper print needs to be large enough for the children to easily read the letters so they do not become frustrated. To make this activity more challenging, ask the children to look for the letters in a child's name or for specific simple words such as "he," "she," "is," "are," and "the."

3. Create a letter-matching game. Print one letter of the alphabet on a piece of paper. Prepare a matching letter on another piece of paper. Make several sets of matching letters. Place the pieces of paper on a table and challenge the children to match the letters you have printed on the pieces of paper. To make this activity simpler, use only three or four letters. You could also cut out letter shapes from sandpaper instead of printing letters on paper.

4. To encourage dramatic play, create a business office. Have telephones, pens, pencils, stamps, and of course lots of paper available for the children to use.

5. Give the children pieces of colored construction paper and invite them to go on a treasure hunt to find items that match the color of the paper.

6. Bring the comic section from a Sunday edition of a newspaper to class. Read a few age-appropriate comic strips to a small group of children. Discuss with the children alternative endings to the comic strips, or ask the children about their favorite comic strip characters.

7. Place some gift-wrap paper with letters of the alphabet printed on it on a table. Challenge a child to touch and then identify a letter. To make this activity more challenging, ask the child to find or name an item that starts with the same sound as the letter identified.

8. Give the children magazines or the sales circulars and advertisements from the Sunday edition of a newspaper. Discuss rhyming words with the children. Show the children an item such as a hat, and challenge the children to find and cut or tear out pictures of things that rhyme with the word hat. For example, they could look for a picture of a cat or a bat. You could also ask the children to look for pictures of things that begin with the same sound as their name. For example, Mike could look for motorcycles, milk, or mattresses, and Latoya could look for lamps, and lollipops. To make this activity simpler, ask the children to look for and cut or tear out pictures that they like. They could also look for items that are a particular color—for example, red or green.

9. Invite the children to make paper name bracelets. Ask a child to decorate a strip of construction paper that has her name printed on it. Then, wrap the paper loosely around her wrist and use a piece of tape to hold the paper ends together. To make this activity more challenging, invite the children to write their names themselves. You could also put all the bracelets on the floor and ask the children to find their own bracelets, or the bracelet of a classmate.

10. Talk about a paper shredder, then visit an office and observe an adult using a paper shredder.

11. As a follow-up activity invite the children to sort two different colors of paper that have been shredded. To make this activity more challenging, use several colors of shredded paper.

12. Invite the children to dictate letters to their parents or friends. Use attractive stationery to encourage the children to participate in this activity. To make this activity more challenging, invite the children who are developmentally ready to write some of the words such as "Dear," "Mom," "Dad," and "Love."

13. Invite the children to use construction paper to make or decorate signs that label items or specific areas of the classroom. For example, the children could help make signs that say "Blocks," "Paper," "Toys," "Book Corner," "Housekeeping," and "Bathroom." Ask the children for their ideas about which signs they would like to make.

14. Place several different pieces of paper on a table for the children to examine. Try to include tissue paper, gift-wrap paper, sandpaper, note pads, and stationery. Discuss with the children how the pieces of paper are alike or different. For example, some of the pieces of paper may be thin, lined, or the same color.

15. Give the children paper and pencils. Encourage the children to print a few letters on the paper. Using phonics, read the letters the children wrote out loud as though they were words. This activity will inspire the children to print more letters as they delight in hearing you read the nonsense words that they are creating.

> This activity will inspire the children to print more letters as they delight in hearing you read the nonsense words that they are creating.

MATHEMATICS

1. Provide graph paper for the children to use.

2. Place several pieces of wallpaper on a table. Use paper that has stripes, or simple clear items such as cars or balls as part of the design. Challenge the children to count the stripes or the number of items on the pieces of paper. To make this activity more challenging, ask the children to order the pieces of paper based on the number of items. For example, the piece of paper with the lowest (smallest) number of cars to the piece of paper with the highest (largest) number of cars.

3. Invite the children to measure different sizes of paper—for example, legal size, letter size, and note paper.

4. Use construction paper to create simple geometric shape puzzles. Cut out a circle shape and then cut it into two equal pieces. Cut out a square shape and cut it into two equal pieces (on the diagonal or straight). Cut out a rectangle shape and cut it into two equal pieces. Place the pieces of paper on a table. Ask the children to put the pieces together to form shapes. This activity helps the children play with geometrical concepts. For example,

> This activity helps the children play with geometrical concepts.

two triangles placed side by side can form a square or a rectangle, two semicircles can form a circle, and two squares placed side by side can form a rectangle. This activity can be made simpler by asking the children to work with only one shape at a time. This activity can be made more challenging by cutting the paper into more than two pieces per geometric shape, or using only one color of construction paper for all of the shapes.

5. Bring the advertisements from the Sunday edition of a newspaper to class. Invite the children to look for and cut or tear out numbers that are printed on the pages. To make this activity more challenging, ask the children to look for and cut or tear out specific numbers. You could also ask the children to look for one 1, two 2s, and three 3s.

6. Challenge the children to fold paper into different shapes—for example, squares or triangles.

7. Prepare a few stacks of different kinds of paper, such as index cards, tissue paper, and sandpaper. Ask the children to estimate how many pieces of paper are in each stack. Then, count the pieces of paper with the children.

8. Challenge the children to cut or tear a piece of paper in half, thirds, etc.

9. Cut out different shapes from pieces of paper and invite the children to create a collage using the different shapes.

10. Draw a number on a piece of construction paper. Invite the children to paste the corresponding number of crumpled pieces of tissue paper on the number. To make this activity more challenging, use higher numbers.

 11. Challenge the children to count the number of pages in a book. To make this activity more challenging, use books with more pages.

12. Place a few almost completely used rolls of paper towels on a table for the children to inspect. Challenge the children to estimate and then count how many paper towels are left on the rolls.

 ## SCIENCE

1. Create a touch table with different samples of paper. Be sure to include books, magazines, newspapers, tissue paper, sandpaper, and wax paper. Encourage the children to handle the paper and talk about how the samples of paper feel.

2. Challenge the children to try to look at a source of light through different types of paper—for example, paper towel, wax paper, tissue paper, newspaper, construction paper, or stationery. Discuss with the children what they see.

3. Invite the children to use water and a plastic eyedropper to wet down different types of paper. Include wax paper, which does not absorb water. Ask the children to observe and then discuss the effect the drops of water have on the different types of paper.

4. On a bright sunny day, invite the children to place a large piece of colored construction paper in a sunny location and then put small items like scissors or unit blocks on top of the paper. For comparison purposes, put another piece of paper with the same items on it in the shade. After several hours, let the children remove the items from the paper and observe the results. The paper that was in the sunlight will have silhouettes of the items that were on the paper. As a result of exposure to sunlight, the color of the paper that was not covered by an item will have faded, creating a silhouette. Allow the children the joy of discovery, and do not tell them what you think might or might not happen.

☺☺☺☺☺☺☺☺☺☺☺☺☺☺☺
Allow the children the joy of discovery, and do not tell them what you think might or might not happen.
☺☺☺☺☺☺☺☺☺☺☺☺☺☺☺

5. Put water in the sensory table. Encourage the children to put different types of paper in the water and observe what happens.

6. Shadow puppet shows are a popular form of entertainment in Indonesia. Invite the children to make shadow puppets using construction paper. The puppets can be simple shapes. Let the children use a hole-punch to decorate their puppets. Attach each puppet to the end of a tongue depressor. Invite the children to make shadows with their puppets by standing between a source of light and a sheet, or a source of light and a wall. Encourage the children to move their puppets first toward and then away from the source of light and observe what happens to the size of the shadows.

7. Place samples of paper on a table. Include sandpaper, tissue paper, and stationery. Give the children a magnifying glass and ask them to closely inspect the different types of paper.

8. Invite the children to make paper airplanes from different types of paper and observe how well they fly. To make this activity more challenging, ask the children to see if they can determine which paper airplanes go the highest or the farthest. Try flying the planes indoors and outdoors.

9. Create a touch matching game using different grades of sandpaper.

10. Encourage the children to listen to the sounds that are made as they rub different grades of sandpaper on different pieces of wood.

11. Invite the children to test the absorption quality of different papers by trying to clean up some spilled water using stationery, wax paper, tissue paper, paper towels, and construction paper.

12. Invite the children to help you make papier-mâché items. Encourage the children to use their sense of touch, and then let them discover how the soft paper becomes hard after several hours.

13. Invite the children to tear or crumple different kinds of paper and listen to the sounds that they make.

14. Encourage the children to use water to make handprints on different pieces of paper—for example, tissue paper, stationery, sandpaper, and butcher paper.

Invite the children to examine the pieces of paper when they are dry and discuss what they see.

15. Encourage the children to experiment by mixing colors on wax paper. Add red, blue, and yellow food coloring to small clear plastic cups of water. Prepare one cup for each color. Place the cups with the colored water, a plastic eyedropper, and some wax paper on a table. Encourage the children to use the eyedropper to put the different colors of water on the wax paper. Discuss with the children what happens when the different colors are mixed together, such as when the blue-colored water is mixed with the red-colored water.

SOCIAL STUDIES

1. Ask the children to bring a piece of paper from their home to class. Discuss with the children the different types of papers that are brought in.

2. Invite the children to create and display a large paper banner showing their appreciation for someone who works at the school such as a bus driver or nurse.

3. Expose the children to the sounds of another language. Invite someone in to read a short children's book that is written in another language. Translate after each paragraph.

4. Organize a paper recycling project in your class.

5. Invite a family member or someone else to class to do an origami demonstration.

6. Gather a collection of business cards and invite the children to examine them. Discuss with the children the different types of work people do. If appropriate, invite family members to send in business cards and display them on a bulletin board.

7. Visit an office supply store and look at all the different kinds of paper.

8. To encourage dramatic play, provide paper tags and other props for a tag sale. Invite the children to make play money out of construction paper.

9. Invite someone in to do a Chinese paper-cutting demonstration.

10. Invite the children to help decorate a large piece of butcher paper to be used as a tablecloth. Then, invite some friends in for a special snack.

11. Visit a supermarket and look at all the different signs and posters in the store.

12. Visit a stationery store and look at the books filled with samples of the different kinds of paper people can order.

PHYSICAL DEVELOPMENT

1. Invite the children to create paper chains of different lengths. You could also measure the chains, and if the children are willing you could combine the chains to form one giant chain.

2. Put shredded paper in the sensory table (without water), and invite the children to play with it.

3. Tape a long piece of butcher paper to the floor. Invite the children to remove their shoes and walk, run, slide, or crawl on the paper. Then, ask the children to put their shoes back on and try to walk on the paper without making a sound.

4. Encourage the children to tear different types of paper into little pieces, and discuss how hard or easy it is to do.

5. Have materials available for the children to make paper kites from different types of paper and fly them.

6. Invite the children to crumple paper into balls. Then, challenge the children to throw or kick the paper balls.

7. Challenge the children to walk from Point A to Point B while balancing a piece of paper on their head. You could also ask the children to walk backward or sideways.

8. Ask the children to make gift-wrap paper to wrap a surprise gift for someone that works at your school.

CREATIVITY

1. Ask the children for ideas about how we can use shredded paper.

2. Staple together a few sheets of blank paper (about 4" × 6") and invite the children to illustrate or dictate stories to create their own books.

3. Show the children a few comic strips, but do not read them. Ask the children to select a comic strip they like and then make up a story using that comic strip.

4. Play some music. Invite the children to dance while holding crepe paper streamers.

5. Read *Yoko's Paper Cranes* by Rosemary Wells. Then, invite the children to create very simple origami figures of their own.

6. Encourage the children to cut or tear paper to create new and unusual shapes of their own.

7. Ask the children to discuss their ideas about what we can do with newspaper after it has been read. For example, some people use newspaper to line the bottom of a birdcage.

8. Invite the children to decorate the papier-mâché items that they made.

9. Invite the children to examine a large piece of paper. Discuss with the children the different things that can be done with a piece of paper.

10. Invite the children to paint on large pieces of butcher paper.

11. Put pieces of paper in the block corner.

12
Ribbons

Ribbons in someone's hair, tied around a gift box, as a border on a blanket, or as a decoration on a piece of clothing are colorful and attractive. They are inexpensive, readily available, and come in many different colors, designs, textures, and widths. Children will really enjoy seeing and handling all the varieties of ribbons.

HELP CHILDREN DISCOVER

1. Ribbons are made from different materials.

2. Ribbons come in different colors and textures. Some ribbons have patterns or designs on them.

3. Ribbons come in different widths.

4. Ribbons can be used in many different ways—for example, to decorate hair, clothing, and presents.

5. Ribbons are flexible and can be tied or folded in different ways.

6. Ribbons can be long or short. Ribbons are stored on spools and cut to whatever length is needed.

7. Some ribbons have a special meaning (awards, medals).

LITERACY

1. Give the children pieces of ribbon and invite them to go on a treasure hunt to look for items that match the color of the ribbon. This activity can be made more challenging by giving the children pieces of ribbon with two or more colors.

2. Create a color-matching game where the children can match the colors of different pieces of ribbon to a picture. For example, look for the color of a green ribbon in a copy of a painting by Van Gogh or in an illustration in a book.

3. Create a letter-matching game. Make a board by dividing a piece of construction paper into four equal sections. In each of the sections, paste a piece of ribbon.

Use ribbons that do not have designs or more than one color. Write the color of each ribbon just below the ribbon. I suggest you start with red, green, blue, and yellow ribbons. Write the letters of the alphabet on index cards. Print one letter per card. Ask the children to pick an index card and find the matching letter on the board. If there is a match, they can cover that ribbon with a token. When all the ribbons are covered with tokens, the game is over. This activity can be made simpler by having index cards with only the letters used on the board. For this example, the letters would be r, e, d, b, 1, u, g, n, y, 1, o, w. The children may realize that the letter e is used in all of the color names on this board. This game can be made even simpler by having the children look for only the first letter of the color. That would limit the letters to r, b, y, g. You also could adjust the index card selections to include a free choice or several duplicates of common letters. To make this activity more challenging, you could provide a board with six different colors of ribbon. You could also use uppercase and lowercase letters.

4. Invite the children to use pieces of ribbon to help you make a large letter on the floor. Discuss with the children the sound of the letter and words that begin with the sound of the letter. Then, challenge the children to go and find things that begin with the sound of that letter and place those things on the floor next to the letter. For example, use ribbon to make the letter M and then encourage the children to find things such as mittens, markers, or magazines and place them by the letter on the floor.

5. Show the children an award ribbon. Discuss with the children what it could represent. For example, winning a race, best dog in show, perfect attendance, or most improved.

6. Give the children pieces of ribbon to use as bookmarks.

7. Cut several different ribbons into two or three pieces each. Place the ribbons on a table and invite the children to find the pieces of ribbon that match.

8. Invite the children to use scraps of ribbon to form the first letter of their name on a piece of paper or on the floor. To make this activity more challenging, suggest that the children make other letters of the alphabet. For those children who are ready, you can write simple words such as Mom or Hat on a card and ask the children to use pieces of ribbon to make the letters for those words.

9. To encourage dramatic play, set up a ribbon store or gift-wrap counter.

10. Create a letter-matching game. Out of the sight of the children, divide a piece of construction paper into four equal parts. In each section, tape one end of a piece of ribbon that is approximately two inches wide and three inches long. Lift the ribbon and print a letter underneath it, then replace the ribbon so the letter is covered. Prepare index cards using the same letters that you printed on the board. Place the index cards on the table so the children can easily see the letters. Invite the children to lift a ribbon and then find the matching letter on an index card. This activity can be made more challenging by asking the children to identify the letter, adding more letters, using uppercase and lowercase letters, or using simple words. You could also use simple patterns such as lines, circles, or squares instead of letters.

11. Invite the children to examine a pair of ballet shoes. Discuss with the children the ribbons on the shoes, and how they are used.

12. Purchase a package of small, assorted stick-on bows. Place the bows on a table and invite the children to sort the bows by color.

13. Place an assortment of ribbons on a table. Invite the children to inspect the ribbons and then talk about how they are alike or different, or what words they would use to describe the different ribbons.

MATHEMATICS

1. Place several pieces of ribbon of different lengths on a table. Challenge the children to order the pieces of ribbon from the shortest to the longest.

2. Tape numbers to the ends of several pieces of ribbon. Place the part of the ribbon with the number on it in a container so it cannot be seen. Drape the other end of the ribbon on the outside of the container. I suggest you use a small plastic pitcher as the container. Invite the children to pull out a ribbon, identify the number taped on the ribbon, and then go and collect that number of tokens, toys, or any other appropriate items. This activity can be made more challenging by using higher numbers or introducing another attribute, such as shape or color.

3. On a table, place a piece of ribbon with a polka dot design on it. Invite the children to count the number of polka dots on the piece of ribbon. This activity can be made more challenging by using a longer piece of ribbon. You could also put a few pieces of ribbon on a table and ask the children to count the number of polka dots on each ribbon and then order the ribbons from the one with the lowest number of polka dots to the one with the highest number. You could also do this activity with any ribbons that have distinct items, such as cars or flowers, as part of their design.

4. Invite the children to measure the lengths of different pieces of ribbon.

5. Cut a ribbon into different length pieces. Be sure there are several pieces that are the same length. Place the pieces on a table or on the floor. Ask the children to pair the pieces of ribbon by their lengths. To make this activity more challenging, use more than one color of ribbon. You could also use ribbons of different widths and ask the children to pair the pieces by their width.

6. Challenge the children to estimate the length of a piece of ribbon on a spool. Invite the children to unwind the ribbon and measure it.

7. Place several ribbons in a clear plastic container. Ask the children to try to estimate how many ribbons are in the container (like guessing the number of jellybeans in a jar). Then, count the ribbons in the container with the children. This activity can be made more challenging by using more ribbons, or asking the children which ribbon in the container is the longest, or the shortest, or how many red ribbons there are.

8. With the help of the children, create a bar graph by cutting ribbons to the height of each child in the class. You could also use ribbons cut to different lengths to create a graph that represents the length of various items such as crayons, books, shoes, or blocks.

9. Ask the children to use large pieces of ribbon to create geometric shapes on a table or on the floor. To make this activity more challenging, invite the children to find items in the room that are the same shape as their ribbon creations and will fit inside them—for example, a rectangular block would be placed inside the outline of a rectangle.

10. Create a pattern-matching game using ribbons. On a table, place a bowl with several pieces of ribbon that are the same size but different colors. Be sure there are several ribbons for each color. Start out with a simple pattern. For example, place a red ribbon and a blue ribbon next to one another on a table, and invite the children to select ribbons from the bowl and match your pattern. This activity can be made more challenging by increasing the number of ribbons you use for the pattern, or by adding more colors of ribbon. In addition, you can place ribbons in different positions, such as having them parallel or forming an X shape. You can also cover the pattern and challenge the children to match your pattern from memory. This is a very complex activity where children are being asked to count, recognize colors, and remember sequences. Keep the patterns simple so you do not ask too much of the children and frustrate them. Another variation on this activity is to give the children the opportunity to create a pattern that you have to replicate. Asking the children to check your work is fun for them and another opportunity for the children to focus on sequencing. On occasion, you may want to make a mistake when you replicate the children's patterns. They just love to correct adults and show them the right way to do something.

> This is a very complex activity where children are being asked to count, recognize colors, and remember sequences. Keep the patterns simple so you do not ask too much of the children and frustrate them.

11. Invite the children to make decorative headbands. Use a tape measure to measure each child's head. Using that measurement (plus a couple of inches for overlap), cut a piece of ribbon to make the headband. Discuss with the children the different-size heads that people have. Measure an adult's head for comparison. Tape the headband so it fits securely.

12. Create a beanbag toss game. Make squares by taping pieces of ribbon to the floor. In each square, write a number. Have a bowl of tokens nearby. Invite a child to toss a beanbag into a square and identify the number in the square. The child can then take the same number of tokens as the number she identified. The game is over when the child has collected a predetermined number of tokens. To make this activity more challenging, use higher numbers.

SCIENCE

1. Put water in the sensory table. Invite the children to speculate about what might happen when pieces of ribbon are put in the water. Ask the children to put the ribbons in the water and then discuss what happens. Do the colors run and change the color of the water? Do the ribbons sink or float?

2. Use ribbons to create a feely board and invite the children to compare the textures of the different ribbons. Be sure to include satin and velvet ribbons.

3. Hang pieces of ribbon from the branches of trees or the top of a fence. Try to place the ribbons in several different locations. Invite the children to observe the ribbons on windy days and on days when there is no wind.

4. Use a ribbon to create a pendulum. Tie a weight such as a few metal washers to one end of a ribbon and then use tape to attach the other end of the ribbon to the edge of a table. Invite the children to swing the pendulum and observe the movement of the pendulum. You can make this activity more interesting by changing both the length of the ribbon and the weight at the end of the pendulum.

5. Place an assortment of ribbons on a table for the children to examine. Ask the children which ribbons belong together. Listen to and accept the children's logic.

6. Place several different ribbons on a table. Invite the children to sort the ribbons by texture.

7. Out of the sight of the children, dip pieces of ribbon in liquids with a distinct scent—for example, coffee, vanilla extract, or liquid soap. Prepare at least two pieces of ribbon for each scent. When the ribbons are dry, invite the children to sort the ribbons by scent.

8. Invite the children to use a magnifying glass to closely inspect several different types of ribbon. Be sure to include satin and velvet ribbons as well as ribbons with patterns on them.

9. Give the children wide pieces of ribbons that are about 10 inches long and have been dipped in water. Ask the children to fold or bend the wet ribbons into circles or other shapes. Use a paper clip or tape to hold each shape in place. Put the ribbons in a Ziploc bag, and place the bag in a freezer. Invite the children to observe and handle the ribbons several hours later. For comparison purposes, also place pieces of dry ribbons in a Ziploc bag, and place that bag in the freezer, too.

10. Create a magnet toy for the children to experiment with. Attach different items such as a metal fork, a plastic fork, a pencil, and a nail, to short and medium lengths of ribbon. Then, attach the pieces of ribbon to the edge of a table or a strip of wood, so the items can dangle freely. Give the children a magnet and invite them to play and experiment.

11. Give each child a piece of ribbon that is about 18 inches long. Ask the children to stand between a source of light and a sheet or a source of light and a wall. Invite the children to experiment and move their ribbons to make dancing, wiggling shadows. Encourage the children to move their ribbons first toward and then away from the source of light and observe what happens to the size of the shadows.

SOCIAL STUDIES

 1. Invite members of the children's families to come in and share stories about any award or special ribbons that they have. You could also invite police officers or firefighters to visit and show the children the ribbons they have on their uniforms, and explain what they represent.

2. Visit a high school and look at the award ribbons in a display case.

3. Invite the children to do a traditional Korean ribbon hat dance. Ask the children to decorate hats and attach a very long ribbon to the top of each hat. Challenge the children to put on the hats and move their heads to try to make the ribbons move in different ways. They can try spinning around, bending at the waist, or moving in any way they choose.

4. Visit a fabric store and look at all the different colors, materials, textures, and widths that ribbons come in.

5. Encourage the children to cooperate with one another. Ask one child to hold a long, extra-wide piece of ribbon by holding one end in each hand. Designate a helper child to find a small item to balance on the ribbon. The child holding the ribbon tries to move from Point A to Point B while balancing the item on the ribbon. The helper child picks up and replaces the item whenever necessary.

6. Visit the gift-wrap department of a store, and watch how bows are made and gifts are wrapped.

7. Invite members of the children's families to class to share with the children any traditional clothing or items that they have that use ribbons.

 8. Kite flying is a popular pastime in China and other countries. Invite the children to make kites, decorate them with ribbons, and fly them.

9. Invite the children to use ribbon to gift-wrap a present such as some cookies or artwork. Give the present to a bus driver, secretary, or anyone else the children may suggest.

PHYSICAL DEVELOPMENT

1. Invite the children to attach bows to boxes.

2. Place pieces of ribbon in an empty tissue box and ask the children to remove one piece of ribbon at a time. To make this activity more challenging, suggest the children use tweezers to remove one piece of ribbon at a time.

3. Punch holes on a piece of cardboard to create a design. Invite the children to thread a piece of ribbon through the holes. To make it easier for the children to thread the ribbon, create a pointed end by wrapping a piece of masking tape around one end of the ribbon.

4. Hang a piece of ribbon in a doorway or on a climbing bar and encourage the children to jump up to tap it.

5. Use large pieces of ribbon to mark off zones on the floor. For each zone, designate a type of movement—for example, jump, slide, crawl, or shake. Invite the children to step into the zones and move accordingly. Stop and start music, clap your hands, or use some other signal to tell the children when to change zones.

6. Use a long piece of ribbon the same way you would a rope, and invite the children to step over it. Raise it in slight increments. You can do the opposite and ask the children to crawl under the ribbon.

7. Give the children pieces of ribbon, and ask them to wiggle the ribbons while listening to different musical selections. Challenge the children to move the ribbon in different ways—for example, up and down, forward and backward, or sideways. To make this activity more interesting you can create a toy for the children to use. Cut several holes in a cottage cheese lid, then thread pieces of ribbon from 5 to 12 inches long through the holes and tie a knot to secure each ribbon. When done, it will look like a jellyfish.

8. Invite the children to decorate Styrofoam or paper plates with ribbons, and then take them outdoors and toss them like Frisbees.

9. Tape a long piece of a wide ribbon to the floor. Challenge the children to walk on the ribbon as though it were a balance beam or a tightrope.

CREATIVITY

1. Encourage the children to handle and examine a short piece and a long piece of ribbon. Ask the children how they would use the ribbons.

2. Discuss with the children ways to use ribbons as a prop when telling a story. For example, the ribbon could be wiggled when talking about rain or the wind.

3. Invite the children to decorate their clothing by taping pieces of ribbon to their shirts.

4. Challenge the children to try and move a piece of ribbon across a table without using their hands. To make this activity more challenging, use ribbons made of different materials and different lengths.

5. Discuss with the children the following problem: "You want to decorate or gift-wrap a present but you do not have any ribbon. What else could you use?"

6. Invite the children to dip pieces of ribbon in paint and create a design on paper. This activity is similar to string painting.

7. Invite the children to create designs by gluing strips of ribbon to paper.

8. Invite the children to dance with a piece of ribbon. To make this activity more challenging, ask two children to hold one piece of ribbon and then dance together.

9. Add pieces of ribbon to the block corner.

13

Shoes and Footwear

Walk into any shoe store and look at all the different kinds of shoes and footwear that are available. It will run the gamut from slippers and simple flip-flops, to boots, and to shoes that have flashing lights, wheels, laces, Velcro, buckles, taps, bows, and bells. If you want even more variety, go to a sporting goods store and examine footwear especially designed for golf, soccer, football, rock climbing, hiking, running, skiing, bowling, skating, and scuba diving. You could also consider shoes designed for specific occupations like construction worker, firefighter, ballet dancer, or tap dancer. Clearly, shoes and footwear, something we all use daily, can be a very interesting topic to explore.

HELP CHILDREN DISCOVER

1. Shoes are made for different purposes.

2. Shoes are made from different materials.

3. Some shoes are designed for particular weather conditions, like sandals or snow boots.

4. Shoes come in different sizes.

5. Some shoes are part of a uniform (firefighter, nurse).

6. Shoes help protect our feet.

7. Shoelaces help keep shoes securely on our feet.

LITERACY

1. Ask the children to remove one of their shoes and toss it into a heap in the middle of the room. Then, invite each child to pick a shoe and locate the rightful owner by finding the matching shoe.

2. Create a game where children can compare the tread of different shoes. Without the children present, carefully dip the soles of different shoes in washable

paint (use only one color) and make prints on pieces of paper. When the paint is dry, place the prints and the shoes used to make the prints on a table or on the floor. Challenge the children to match the prints to the shoes that made the prints.

3. Create a game where the children look for letters on their shoes. For example, challenge the children to find the letter N (Nike) or R (Reebok) on their shoes. To make this activity simpler, print a letter on an index card and ask the children to look for the same letter on their shoes.

4. Out of the sight of the children, trace the outline of several different types of footwear on pieces of paper. For example, trace a swim fin, baby shoe, hiking boot, flip-flop, jogging shoe, and a high heel shoe. Place the footwear and the outlines of the footwear on a table. Challenge the children to find which piece of footwear matches which outline.

5. Place a handful of index cards with letters printed on them in a large shoe or slipper. Place cards with matching letters printed on them face up on a table. Invite the children to reach in the shoe, pull out an index card with a letter on it, then find the card with the matching letter on the table. To make this activity more challenging, use more letters, uppercase and lowercase letters, or ask the children to identify the letter and say a word that begins with the same sound as that letter. This activity can be made simpler by limiting the number of letters or using colors instead of letters.

6. Invite the children to examine a pair of shoes. Ask the children to talk about who might wear the shoes, and what sort of work they might do. Also, discuss with the children why people wear shoes.

7. Discuss with the children the times they think people should not wear shoes—for example, at the beach, in bed, or in the bathtub.

8. Make a lacing card for the children to enjoy. On a piece of cardboard, print a large-size letter. Use a hole-punch to punch holes in the printed letter. Give a child the lacing card and a shoelace and invite him to thread the shoelace through the holes.

 9. Design a game where the children match footwear to sports or recreational activities. Place an assortment of footwear used in sports or recreational activities on a table— for example, running shoes, golf shoes, hiking boots, swim fins, bowling shoes, and ski boots. Place pictures of people wearing that footwear and engaged in those sports or recreational activities on the table. Challenge the children to place the footwear next to the picture that shows someone wearing the footwear or engaged in an activity when the special footwear is used. Discuss with the children the choices they made. A variation on this activity would be to use an assortment of footwear used in different occupations instead of in sports or recreational activities—for example, ballet shoe, construction worker's boot, firefighter's boot, nurse's shoe, shoe covers worn by a surgeon, and shoe covers worn by teachers that work with infants.

10. To encourage dramatic play, create a shoe store.

11. Place several sentence strips in a large boot. Invite a child to pick out a sentence strip. Read the sentence strip and ask the child to finish the sentence. For example, "My shoes are . . . ," "I wear boots when . . . ," "Hiking boots are . . . ," "My Mommy wears shoes that are . . . ." A variation on this activity would be to include sentence strips on other topics. For example, "My name is . . . ," "I like to eat . . . ," "I know how to . . . ," "My favorite toy is . . . ," "I wish I could . . . ."

12. Place a collection of shoes on the floor. Invite the children to sort the shoes by color. To make this activity more challenging, print a color word on a piece of paper, show it to the children, and ask them to find shoes with that color.

13. Invite the children to help write a letter asking permission to visit a dance studio.

14. Discuss with the children the different things that can be used with shoes. For example, a shoe brush, shoehorn, shoetree, and insoles. If possible, have examples of each item for the children to examine.

MATHEMATICS

1. Borrow the measuring tool from a shoe store. Measure each child's feet and determine the correct shoe size. Ask the children to look for the shoe size printed on the inside of their shoes.

2. Place an assortment of shoes and hiking boots on a table. Invite the children to count and compare the number of lace eyelets of the different shoes and hiking boots.

3. Place a variety of shoe and bootlaces of different lengths on the floor or a table. Invite the children to measure the laces and then arrange them by length, from the shortest to the longest. To make this activity simpler, use only a few laces.

4. Invite the children to use shoe length as a way to measure distance. Ask the children to measure the distance from Point A to Point B by placing one foot directly in front of the other and counting their steps as they move. Create a chart. As each child does this activity, record the child's name and the number of steps (shoe length) she used. Be sure an adult participates in this activity. After everyone has had a turn, look at the chart and compare the number of shoe lengths each person used.

5. Encourage the children to estimate how many ping-pong balls will fit in the shoe of an adult. Count the ping-pong balls as the children place them in the shoe. For comparison, then do the same thing using a child's shoe, and then using a boot. This activity can be made simpler by using larger objects, such as tennis balls. It can be made more challenging by using smaller objects, such as crayons or tokens.

6. Place an assortment of shoes on a table and invite the children to order the shoes from the shortest to the longest or from the narrowest to the widest.

7. Invite the children to remove their shoes and place them in a long line from Point A to Point B. Measure the length of the line they created, or count the number of shoes in the line. To avoid confusion when this activity is completed, I suggest taping the children's names to the soles of their shoes.

☺☺☺☺☺☺☺☺☺☺☺☺☺☺
To avoid confusion when this activity is completed, I suggest taping the children's names to the soles of their shoes.
☺☺☺☺☺☺☺☺☺☺☺☺☺☺

8. Invite the children to arrange a collection of different boots from the shortest to the tallest.

9. With the children, create a graph of the colors of their shoes.

10. Invite the children to order an assortment of shoes by the height of the heels on the shoes.

11. Invite the children to count the number of cleats on a soccer or golf shoe.

12. Place an assortment of different footwear on a table. Include slippers, flip-flops, and hiking boots. Challenge the children to order the footwear by weight from the lightest to the heaviest.

13. Place an assortment of shoelaces on the floor. Encourage the children to use the laces to create geometric shapes such as squares and triangles. To make this activity simpler, give the children pieces of paper with the outline of geometric shapes drawn on them, and ask the children to place laces on the outlined shapes.

14. Use large bootlaces to form circles or other geometric shapes, such as triangles or rectangles, on the floor. In each shape, place a piece of paper with a number written on it. Place a collection of shoes nearby. Challenge the children to put the number of shoes in the geometric shape corresponding to the number written on the piece of paper. To make this activity more challenging, use more bootlaces to make bigger circles or other geometric shapes, and write higher numbers on the pieces of paper. You could also print dots instead of numbers on the pieces of paper.

SCIENCE

1. When outdoors, wet down a section of a paved surface and invite the children to walk on the wet surface and make shoe prints. Ask the children to compare the different treads and sizes of the shoe prints. Challenge the children to see if they can find the teacher's shoe print. Encourage the children to observe as the water evaporates and the prints disappear.

2. Place several pairs of shoes on a table. Take one shoe from each pair. Then, out of the sight of the children, tap a shoe from one of the pairs on a hollow wooden block and ask the children to listen to the sound. Invite the children to identify the mate to the shoe that made the sound. Try to include flip-flops, tap dance shoes, and sport shoes with cleats because they make interesting sounds.

3. Encourage the children to walk barefoot outdoors on different surfaces such as sand, grass, and pebbles. Discuss how it feels to walk on the different surfaces when not wearing shoes. You could also do this indoors by having the children walk barefoot on items such as butcher paper, rug samples, and bubble wrap. Make sure the surfaces are not too hot, and carefully inspect the area for any safety hazards before having the children walk barefoot.

4. A natural follow-up activity would be to ask the children to walk on different surfaces when they are wearing shoes. Ask the children to listen to the sounds that the shoes make when walking on different surfaces. When the children are wearing shoes, they could also walk on leaves and mulch.

5. Invite the children to handle an assortment of shoes and group them by material (texture). For example, you can use canvas, suede, leather, and rubber shoes.

6. Encourage the children to use a magnifying glass to examine the heels and soles of different shoes. In addition to noticing tread patterns, ask the children to check for grass, sand, or other interesting things that might be stuck to the bottoms of the shoes.

7. Place an assortment of shoes and pictures of different weather conditions such as rain and snow on a table. Ask the children to select the shoes they would wear for each weather condition, and place that shoe by the corresponding picture.

8. Invite the children to compare the flexibility of the soles of different footwear. For example, ask the children to compare and discuss the soles of slippers, hiking boots, jogging shoes, flip-flops, and ballet shoes.

9. When outdoors, scatter some sand on a paved surface and then invite the children to walk or slide on the sand. Ask the children to listen to the sounds their shoes make while walking or sliding on the sand. Then, discuss with the children if shoes with different soles make different sounds.

10. Give the children a flashlight and in a place with minimum light encourage them to examine shoes with and without reflective tape on them. Discuss with the children why some shoes have reflective tape on them.

11. Place a collection of shoelaces on a table. Invite the children to sort the laces. Discuss with the children the logic they used to sort the laces.

SOCIAL STUDIES

1. Ask the children to bring in a shoe or slipper from home. Encourage the children to talk about who wears the shoe, and when the person wears it.

2. Invite family members to class to share special footwear that they use. For example, shoes designed for work, dancing (flamenco, clogging, tap, ballet), or sports activities (hiking, rock climbing). This activity may provide a positive way to discuss shoes designed for people with special needs.

This activity may provide a positive way to discuss shoes designed for people with special needs.

3. Invite family members to class to share footwear that are part of a traditional costume. If possible, invite someone of Japanese descent to talk about traditional Japanese shoes, and the custom of removing shoes before entering a home.

4. Place a doormat by the door that leads to the playground. Encourage the children to help keep the building clean by using the doormat before entering the building.

5. Encourage the children to cooperate and help one another put on boots.

6. Visit a shoe repair shop. Look at the different kinds of soles and heels that are used to repair shoes.

7. Visit a dance studio or invite a dancer to your class.

8. Invite a firefighter to class to show and talk about the boots that she uses.

9. Invite someone who goes fly-fishing to class. Ask him to bring his waders to class.

10. Visit a sporting goods store and examine the footwear.

11. As a way to say thank you for all that they do for the school, encourage the children to offer to brush the shoes of the staff in the office or the kitchen.

12. Visit a shoeshine stand and watch as a pair of shoes are shined.

13. Visit a pet store and examine shoes that are made for dogs.

PHYSICAL DEVELOPMENT

1. Invite the children to lace shoes.

2. Create a game where you invite the children to toss shoes into three different laundry baskets. Place one basket in the middle, one on the right, and one on the left. Count how many shoes went into each basket.

3. Have high heels and large boots available for the children to try to walk in.

4. Invite the children to use a shoe brush or shoeshine cloth on their shoes.

5. Challenge the children to walk, walk backward, slide, or run from Point A to Point B while balancing a crayon or small object on a flip-flop or sandal that they are holding in their hands.

6. Challenge the children to move an empty shoe or boot, using a rhythm stick, double unit block, or slat board from Point A to Point B.

7. Challenge the children to walk on a balance beam barefoot, then when wearing shoes.

8. Invite the children to kick a soft beach ball when barefoot, and then when wearing shoes. With the children, measure and compare the distance the ball traveled on each occasion.

9. Encourage the children to experiment with walking. Invite the children to walk slowly, quickly, silently, on tiptoes, and on heels. Ask for their suggestions as to how to walk.

CREATIVITY

1. Solicit the children's ideas for inventing a new style of shoe.

2. Invite the children to put shoes on their hands and create a dance with their new "feet."

3. Invite the children to walk in slightly dampened sand or mud and use their shoes (footprints) to create patterns in the sand. You could also have available items such as small boxes that can fit over the children's shoes for them to use to make different patterns.

4. Pose a problem to the children and listen to their solutions. "Pretend you went for a long walk. You took your shoes off to rest your feet, but when it was time to go home you could not find your shoes. How would you get home? What could you do to keep your feet from getting hurt or sore?" Accept the children's responses, which may range from "I would call Daddy to carry me home" to "I would just grow wings and fly home" or "I would find an airplane to ride home" or "I would wait for someone to come get me" or "I would just get another pair of shoes." Remember this is an exercise in creativity, not practicality.

5. Encourage the children to decorate their shoes. Ask the children to suggest what materials they could use. Be sure the decorations are made from materials that can be easily removed, such as ribbons or colored tape.

6. Invite the children to try on a pair of magic shoes that helps them become anyone or anything they want. Talk about their choices.

7. Play some music and invite the children to create a ballet, tap, or modern dance.

14
Spoons

There is more variety to spoons than meets the eye. Spoons come in several different sizes. There are tiny demitasse spoons, teaspoons, tablespoons, serving spoons, and several varieties of large mixing spoons. There are also some special-purpose spoons like measuring spoons, long-handled ice cream soda spoons, and small spoons for feeding babies. Spoons can be made from many different materials including bone, gold, silver, plastic, wood, and stainless steel. Plastic spoons are inexpensive and come in several different colors. For some of the activities, you may need to remind the children not to put the spoons in their mouths.

HELP CHILDREN DISCOVER

1. Spoons come in many different sizes.

2. Spoons are made from different materials.

3. Some spoons have interesting designs on their handles.

4. There are spoons that are designed for a special purpose such as eating soup, measuring ingredients, cooking, or serving food.

LITERACY

1. Gather a collection of spoons with different patterns on the handles. Be sure to have at least two of each pattern. Place the spoons on a table and invite the children to sort the spoons using the patterns on the handles.

2. Out of the sight of the children, trace the outline of several different spoons on a piece of paper. Place the spoons used to make the outlines and the piece of paper on a table. Challenge the children to place each spoon on the matching outline.

3. Place several different-colored plastic spoons on a table. Challenge the children to sort the plastic spoons by color.

4. Pour a box of alphabet cookies into a pie tin. Give each child a spoon and invite the children to use the spoons to scoop out the letters of their name

and put them on a paper plate or a napkin. When complete, the children can eat their names. To make this activity simpler, give the children a card with their name printed on it, and ask them to scoop out the matching letters.

5. As a follow-up activity, print letters of the alphabet on index cards. Print one letter on each card. Ask the children to pick a card and then try to use a spoon to scoop out the same letter from a pie tin filled with alphabet cookies, and place it on a napkin. To make this activity more challenging, ask the children to identify the letter and say a word that starts with the same sound as the letter they identified. You could also print simple words like "stop," "go," or "red" on the index cards instead of letters. Of course, when the activity is finished, the children should be able to consume the letters they have scooped out of the pie tin.

6. Prepare a recipe chart for making brownies. Invite the children to follow the directions and help make the brownies by stirring the mixture with a large spoon. Depending on the recipe, the batter may need to be stirred 40 or more strokes. Count the strokes with the children. It might be easier for the children to count to 10 four times.

7. Place an assortment of spoons on a table for the children to handle. Discuss with the children how the spoons are alike, and how the spoons are different.

8. To encourage dramatic play, set up a restaurant, complete with menus, dishes, spoons, and a cash register.

 9. Create a matching game with pictures of food and eating utensils. On a table, place pictures of different foods and an assortment of spoons. Challenge the children to place the correct spoon next to a picture of the food eaten with that spoon. For example, a teaspoon next to a cup of tea, a soupspoon by a bowl of soup, or a serving spoon next to a large bowl of mashed potatoes. To make this activity more challenging, you could add forks and chopsticks and pictures of foods that are eaten with forks and chop sticks.

10. Invite the children to use a soupspoon to eat alphabet soup and challenge the children to identify letters as they eat.

11. Discuss with the children the foods that they like to eat with spoons.

12. Read the book *Stone Soup* by Marcia Brown. Invite the children to make soup. Use measuring spoons to measure the ingredients, large spoons to stir the soup, and soupspoons to eat the soup. As always, any activities involving the use of a stove require careful and constant adult supervision.

13. Invite the children to dramatize the story of *Goldilocks and the Three Bears*. Use a large bowl and spoon, a medium bowl and spoon, and a small bowl and spoon as props.

14. Create a color-matching game. Divide a sheet of construction paper into four equal sections. Paste a red rectangle cut from construction paper in one section, and blue, green, and yellow rectangles in the remaining sections. Place

several red, blue, green, and yellow plastic spoons on a table. Invite the children to place each spoon in the section with the rectangle that matches the color of the spoon. This game can be made more challenging if you print the words of the colors instead of using pieces of colored construction paper.

MATHEMATICS

1. Place an assortment of different kinds of spoons on a table. Invite the children to order the spoons by size from the smallest to the largest.

2. Place a large bowl of Cheerios on a table. Give each child a spoon and a small paper plate. Invite the children to fill the spoon with Cheerios, place them on the plate, count them, and of course eat them. To make this activity more challenging, ask the children to use larger spoons such as serving spoons, or put out smaller pieces of food such as green peas.

3. Create a matching game. Divide a piece of construction paper into four sections. In each section, print one of the following: $\frac{1}{8}, \frac{1}{4} \frac{1}{2}$. Give the children an assortment of measuring spoons and ask them to look at the fractions printed on the spoons and then put the spoons in the correct section of the paper.

4. Encourage the children to estimate how many tablespoons of water it would take to fill a small cup. With the children helping, count the number of tablespoons it takes to fill the cup. For example, it takes six tablespoons to fill a three-ounce cup. Use both liquid and solid items, such as water and sand. To make this activity more challenging, use a smaller spoon such as a teaspoon.

5. Create a game using a spinner. Place a spoon and a bowl filled with pebbles in the middle of the table. Give each child a piece of paper that has 10 dots drawn on it. Invite a child to use the spinner. After identifying the number, the child can use the spoon to scoop out the corresponding number of pebbles and place them on the dots. When all the dots are covered with pebbles, the child is done playing the game. To make this activity more challenging, write higher numbers on the spinner and increase the number of dots that need to be covered on the piece of paper.

6. Create a color-pattern matching game using brightly colored plastic spoons. Place an assortment of different-colored plastic spoons in a bowl or on a table. Start with a simple pattern. For example, place a green and a blue spoon next to one another on the table. Invite the children to select spoons and match your pattern. To make this activity more challenging, you can increase the number of spoons used or add more colors. For example, try blue, blue, yellow, or an even more complex pattern such as blue, red, yellow, yellow. Another way to make this activity more challenging is to let the children see the pattern for a moment, then cover it with a piece of paper, and ask the children to recreate the pattern from memory. This is a very complex activity where children are asked to count, recognize colors, and remember sequence. Keep the patterns simple so that you do not ask too much of the children and frustrate them. Another variation on this activity is to give the children the opportunity to create a

pattern that you have to replicate. Asking the children to check your work is fun for them and another opportunity for them to focus on sequencing. On occasion, you may want to make a mistake when you replicate the children's patterns. They just love to correct adults and show them the right way to do something.

7. For snack or lunch, serve a food like mashed potatoes and invite the children to use a serving spoon and serve themselves. Suggest they take two, three, or four spoonfuls. Count each spoonful as they put the food on their plates.

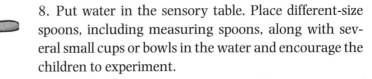

8. Put water in the sensory table. Place different-size spoons, including measuring spoons, along with several small cups or bowls in the water and encourage the children to experiment.

9. Place several different-colored spoons in a bowl or clear plastic container. Invite the children to look carefully, then ask them to estimate how many blue spoons are in the container. Count the blue spoons with the children. To make this activity more challenging, ask the children to estimate the total number of spoons in the container. Then, count all the spoons with the children.

10. With the children, follow the directions for baking or cooking something, and measure the ingredients using measuring spoons.

11. Place a collection of different spoons on a table. Invite the children to measure the length of the handles of the different spoons.

12. Invite the children to create a spoon mobile. Tie a string to a spoon and then fasten the string to a hanger or stick. Do this with different spoons and different lengths of string. This activity presents a good opportunity to talk about balance and weight distribution.

13. In a remote area of the playground, encourage the children to use large spoons to dig a hole. From time to time, measure the depth of the hole as the children dig deeper and deeper.

SCIENCE

1. Invite the children to look at their images in the bowl (the concave side of the spoon that holds the food) of a highly polished large spoon. Ask the children to hold the spoon by the handle with the handle pointed toward the floor. Then, ask the children to rotate the spoon, and look at their images again (be sure they keep the handle pointed toward the floor). Discuss with the children if they see any difference in the images. Encourage the children to be observant

and experiment by slowly moving the spoon back and forth. The concave shape of the bowl of the spoon will cause the image to be distorted and upside down. On the rounded (convex) side, the image will be distorted and right side up.

2. Invite the children to experiment, and tap different surfaces such as wood, rocks, bowls, metal pots, or cardboard boxes with plastic, wooden, and metal spoons. Encourage the children to listen to the different sounds that the spoons make. You could also ask the children to listen as they drop spoons made of different materials onto various surfaces—for example, counter tops, carpet, and tile and wood floors.

> The concave shape of the bowl of the spoon will cause the image to be distorted and upside down. On the rounded (convex) side, the image will be distorted and right side up.

3. With the children, place a wooden, plastic, and metal spoon vertically into a cup of very cold water. Be sure the handles of the spoons are above the water line. After a few minutes, encourage the children to touch the handles of the spoons and describe how they feel compared to how they felt before. You could also place the spoons in the freezer for an hour. Remove the spoons and place them on a table. Ask the children to look at the spoons carefully. Does the metal spoon look different after a few moments? (It might be frost covered.) Then, ask the children to touch the spoons and talk about how the spoons feel. Metal is a better conductor of cold than wood or plastic.

4. Place an assortment of spoons made of different materials on a table near a window where sunbeams are shining into the room. Invite the children to use several different spoons to try to catch and reflect the sunlight onto a nearby wall. Let the children discover that shiny (highly polished) spoons work best.

5. Place an assortment of spoons and a magnet on a table. Invite the children to use the magnet to experiment with and discover which spoons are attracted to (stick to) the magnet. Encourage the children to check both the bowl and handle portion of the spoons because they can be made of different materials.

6. Suspend several spoons made of different materials from a hanger. To do this, use pieces of string that are 10 to 12 inches long, and tie the spoons to the hanger so they are two inches apart. Invite the children to tap or knock the spoons together and then listen to the sounds that they make.

7. Put water in the sensory table. Give the children spoons made of different materials. Ask the children to experiment and determine which spoons sink and which spoons float.

8. While the children are using finger paint, invite them to use a spoon to sprinkle some sand on the paint. Encourage the children to discuss what they feel and how the sand changes the texture of the paint.

9. Invite the children to use a spoon to stir a few drops of food coloring into a dense (thick) liquid such as cake batter. Ask the children to observe and discuss what happens as they stir. For comparison, you might want to ask the children to try the same activity using dry ingredients, such as salt or sand, or less-dense liquids, such as water or club soda.

10. Invite the children to use a magnifying glass to look for letters on the handles of spoons. The manufacturer's name or logo, or the place the spoon was made, is often printed on the underside of the handles.

11. Outdoors, fill a bucket with water. Give the children different-size spoons and ask them to experiment by using the spoons to stir the water in different ways. Encourage the children to observe the effect that stirring has on the water, and what effect, if any, the size of the spoon has on the stirring. If the children stir the water quickly enough, they may be able to create small whirlpools.

12. Create a xylophone for the children to experiment with. Roll two towels and place them parallel to one another, about six inches apart. Lay four or five spoons made of different materials across the rolled towels so that it looks like a xylophone. Invite the children to tap the spoons with a rhythm stick or other object and listen to the sounds that are made.

SOCIAL STUDIES

1. Ask the children to bring to class a spoon from their home. Discuss with the children the different kinds of spoons that they brought to school or have in their home.

2. Invite someone in to make spoon bread with the children.

3. Invite in or visit a baby and watch as an adult feeds the baby using a baby spoon.

4. Make pudding with the children and invite the children from the room next door, or people in the office to join you for a treat. Ask the children to set the table with napkins and spoons.

5. Bake some muffins with the children. Ask the children to cooperate and take turns as they stir the batter with a spoon. Some prepared muffin mixes need to be stirred 50–75 times. Be sure to keep count.

6. Visit the housewares department of a store and look at spoons. Notice the different patterns on the handles, and the different colors and materials used to make handles.

7. Visit a pharmacy or the make-up counter of a department store to see the tiny spoons that they use.

8. To encourage cooperation and social interaction, set up an ice cream store in the dramatic play area.

9. Visit the kitchen of a restaurant or the school cafeteria and look for different kinds of spoons.

10. Visit a bakery. Ask the children to notice the spoons that the bakers use.

11. Visit a high school chemistry lab and ask for a demonstration of how chemists use spoons.

PHYSICAL DEVELOPMENT

1. Invite the children to eat cereal or ice cream using spoons.

2. Put water in the sensory table. Place small items in the water. Invite the children to use regular and slotted spoons to try to remove the items from the water.

3. Challenge the children to nest a group of spoons. Count how many they can nest before they fall over.

4. Out of the sight of the children, bury some small items in sand. Give the children spoons and invite them to dig for treasure.

5. Ask the children to walk from Point A to Point B while balancing a pebble or other small object on a spoon. To make this activity more challenging, use a larger item or a smaller spoon. You could also ask the children to slide or walk backward.

6. Hang a large spoon in a doorway and encourage the children to jump up and tap it.

7. Invite the children to use a large spoon to hit a ball made of crumpled paper.

8. Fill the sensory table with sand. Out of the sight of the children, place spoons, forks, and some other items under the sand. Encourage the children to reach in the sand and use their sense of touch to pull only the spoons out of the sand.

CREATIVITY

1. Discuss with the children the different things we could use a spoon for other than eating. For example, we could use spoons to dig in a garden or stir paint.

2. Invite the children to spread paint with spoons.

3. Ask the children to solve a problem. Pretend they want to eat some pudding, but do not have a spoon. What would they do? Accept the children's responses. Remember, we are trying to stimulate creative thinking and neatness does not count.

> **Remember, we are trying to stimulate creative thinking, and neatness does not count.**

4. Add several different-size spoons to the sand box.

5. Invite the children to use spoons to tap out rhythms.

6. Encourage the children to make print designs with slotted and other spoons that have been dipped in paint.

7. Place spoons in the block corner.

8. Ask the children to create a game that involves using a spoon, or ask them to discuss how they could use a spoon as a toy.

9. Place a spoon on the floor and ask the children to move it from Point A to Point B without using their hands.

15

Toilet Paper and Other Cardboard Rolls

It is a private little secret, but if the truth be told, I have never met a preschool teacher that did not collect toilet paper rolls. Teachers know that with a little imagination they can be used in many creative ways. If you expand your collection to include rolls for paper towels, aluminum foil, and Saran wrap, and large rolls from butcher or gift-wrap paper, you can do even more.

HELP CHILDREN DISCOVER

1. Cardboard rolls come in different sizes.

2. Fabrics, carpet, and linoleum are stored on cardboard rolls.

3. Cardboard rolls make it easy to dispense items such as paper and aluminum foil.

4. Cardboard rolls are used to store and ship documents, posters, prints, and paintings.

5. Cardboard rolls come in different thicknesses. Some are very sturdy.

LITERACY

1. Play "I spy." Give each child a paper towel roll and invite the children to use the rolls as telescopes. Challenge the children to look through their rolls to locate and identify items that are a particular color, such as something that is blue. To make this activity more challenging, you can ask the children look for items that begin with the same sound as the letter B, or any other letter you wish to use. You could also ask the children to look for items that rhyme with a particular word.

2. Invite the children to use a cardboard roll as a megaphone when reciting a familiar poem or joining in the refrain of a favorite book such as *Brown Bear, Brown Bear, What Do You See?* by Bill Martin.

3. Use a paper towel roll to create a scroll. Attach a long piece of paper (three feet or more) to a paper towel roll. Invite the children to decorate the edges of the paper. Then, ask the children to create a story that you can write on the paper. When done, roll the paper around the cardboard roll. Unroll the paper as you or the children read or tell the story. You could also ask the children to draw or dictate original stories for their own individual scrolls.

4. Seal one end of a cardboard roll with paper and tape. Create a die that has letters printed on it instead of numbers. Invite the children to place the die in the cardboard roll, shake it, and pour the die out onto the table. Challenge the children to identify the letter on the die and then to find items that start with the same sound as the letter identified. For example, for the letter T the children could find a toy, tie, or telephone. You could also use pictures of items for the children to point to instead of looking for items in the room.

5. On a table, place a rolling pin, dowel, round crayon, and some cardboard rolls. Ask the children to handle the items and discuss how they are similar and how they are different. You could also ask the children what words (adjectives) they could use to describe the items.

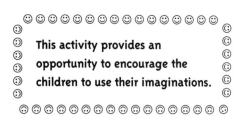

This activity provides an opportunity to encourage the children to use their imaginations.

6. Invite the children to pretend to go stargazing. Seal one end of a toilet paper roll with paper and tape. Make random pinholes in the paper. Ask the children to look through the roll toward a source of light such as a lamp. Encourage the children to talk about what they see and what the points of light remind them of. This activity provides an opportunity to encourage the children to use their imaginations.

7. Create a matching game. Seal one end of a toilet paper roll with paper and tape. Paste a piece of red construction paper on the roll. Do the same thing with other rolls using a different color of construction paper for each roll. Place the rolls and scraps of different-colored construction paper on a table. Invite the children to put each scrap of construction paper into the roll that has a matching piece of construction paper pasted on it. This activity can be made more challenging by printing the word for the color on the roll instead of using a piece of colored construction paper.

8. Invite the children to decorate a cardboard roll and create a magic wand. Encourage the children to use the magic wand as a prop in dramatic play.

9. Invite the children to create hand puppets by decorating toilet paper rolls with yarn and markers. Then, encourage the children to put on a puppet show

10. Create a find the letter game. To make the game board, print a few letters scattered in different locations on a piece of construction paper. Each letter needs to be small enough so it can be hidden when one end of a toilet paper roll is placed on top of it. Give each child a board and a toilet paper roll. Say a letter and challenge the children to find that letter on the paper and hide it (cover it) with their toilet paper roll. This activity can be made simpler by showing the children a letter rather than saying it. It can be made more challenging by

using uppercase and lowercase letters, or by asking the children to say a word that begins with that letter.

11. Create a letter-recognition game. Make a fishing pole by attaching a string with a magnet tied at one end to a 12-inch cardboard roll. Write letters of the alphabet on 3" × 5" index cards (one letter per card). Fasten a large metal paper clip to each card, and place the cards on the floor with the letters clearly visible. Invite a child to go fishing for specific letters, like B or G. This activity can be made simpler by limiting the number of letters used or by having an adult identify the letters the children catch. To make this activity more challenging, increase the number of letters, or ask the children to fish for the letters in their names or in simple words like "red" or "blue."

12. Put out several different cardboard rolls for the children to use when working with play dough. Discuss with the children the different patterns and designs they can make using the cardboard rolls.

MATHEMATICS

1. Place an assortment of cardboard rolls on a table. Invite the children to dip the ends of the rolls in paint and use them to make circle prints on a piece of paper. Encourage the children to compare the different diameters (widths) of the circles. You could also ask the children to look for the largest or smallest circles that they made. This activity provides an opportunity to talk about size, circumference, and diameter.

> **This activity provides an opportunity to talk about size, circumference, and diameter.**

2. Place cardboard rolls on the floor. Challenge the children to use the rolls to make geometric shapes such as triangles, squares, and rectangles.

3. Collect a few almost completely used rolls of paper towels. Challenge the children to estimate and then count how many paper towels are left on the rolls.

4. Seal one end of a cardboard roll using paper and tape. Invite the children to guess how many crayons will fit inside the roll. Then, ask the children to count the crayons as they put them in the roll. This activity can be made more challenging by using smaller objects or a wider or longer cardboard roll.

5. Place an assortment of cardboard rolls on a table. Invite the children to order the cardboard rolls by diameter.

6. Place an assortment of cardboard rolls on a table. Invite the children to measure the lengths of the different cardboard rolls. Ask the children to determine which cardboard roll is the shortest and which is the longest.

7. Ask the children to fill various cardboard rolls with different items such as rocks and tissues. Use construction paper and tape to seal both ends of the rolls. Then, ask the children to order the cardboard rolls from the lightest to the heaviest.

8. Create a counting game. Place a bowl of tokens in the center of a table. Seal one end of a cardboard roll with construction paper and tape. Invite a child to

place a die in the cardboard roll, shake it, and then pour the die out onto the table. Challenge the child to identify the number on the die and then select the same number of tokens as the die indicates. The game is over when the child has 10 tokens. To make this activity more challenging, use more than one die.

9. On the floor, place a number of different-size items and several toilet paper and other cardboard rolls. Invite the children to tell you what items they think will fit inside which rolls. Then, ask the children to place the items in the rolls.

10. Cut geometric shapes such as triangles and squares out of a sturdy cardboard roll. Invite the children to dip the rolls in paint and then roll them on paper to make shape prints.

11. Invite the children to use paper towel rolls to measure the distance from Point A to Point B. Ask the children to count the number of rolls that are needed. You could also measure the same distance using gift-wrap paper rolls or toilet paper rolls.

SCIENCE

1. Make kazoos for the children to experiment with. Use a rubber band to fasten wax paper to one end of a toilet paper roll. Prepare one kazoo for each child. Invite the children to talk into their cardboard roll kazoos. Encourage the children to gently touch the wax paper while talking to feel the vibration. Repeat this activity using other kinds of paper. Encourage the children to listen carefully as they talk into the kazoos made with different kinds of paper. Then, ask the children to talk about what they heard.

2. With the children, put some water and food coloring in a clear plastic cup. Use a little less than half a cup of water. Place a cardboard roll vertically in the water so at least half of the cardboard roll is above the water line. After a few minutes invite the children to look at the cardboard roll, but do not move it. Check it again in an hour, and after several hours or the next day. Encourage the children to notice how far up the cardboard roll the liquid has traveled. This activity provides an opportunity for the children to observe capillary action.

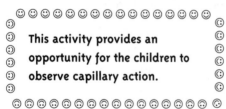

This activity provides an opportunity for the children to observe capillary action.

3. With the children, soak some toilet paper rolls in water. After a few minutes, remove the toilet paper rolls from the water. Encourage the children to examine the wet toilet paper rolls. Then, place some of the rolls in a Ziploc bag and place them in the freezer. Put the other rolls on a plate and leave them on a table. After an hour or more, remove the toilet paper rolls from the freezer. Encourage the children to examine all the toilet paper rolls and talk about any differences they see or feel between the rolls that were put in the freezer and the ones that were not put in the freezer.

4. With the help of the children, fill various cardboard rolls with different items such as small toys, sand, paper, nails, or pebbles. Seal both ends of the rolls and

invite the children to shake the rolls and listen to the sounds that the rolls make. Ask the children to order the rolls from the loudest to the softest sounds. You could also vary the quantity of items or the length of the cardboard rolls, and ask the children if they can hear any difference in the sounds that the rolls make. A variation on this activity would be to fill cardboard rolls with the same items. Out of the sight of the children, make at least two cardboard rolls for each item used. Ask the children to shake the rolls and match the cardboard rolls by the sounds that the rolls make.

5. Cover one end of several toilet paper rolls with different materials such as cellophane, lace, aluminum foil, tissue paper, or construction paper. Invite the children to look at a light such as a lamp through the rolls. Discuss what the children see. This activity provides an opportunity to introduce the words opaque, transparent, and translucent.

6. Set up an incline board or use the slide on the playground. With the children, fill toilet paper rolls with different items and seal both ends of the rolls. Invite the children to speculate as to which toilet paper roll will move down the board the fastest. Ask the children to observe as the toilet paper rolls move down the board. If possible, change the angle of incline of the board and repeat the activity.

7. Invite the children to tap empty cardboard rolls of different lengths and diameters with rhythm sticks and listen to the different sounds that they make. You could also ask the children to put some items into cardboard rolls—for example, cotton balls or crayons—and then seal the rolls. Invite the children to tap both the empty rolls and the ones that have been filled. Encourage the children to listen carefully to determine if the sounds made when tapping the rolls with items in them are different from the sounds made when tapping rolls that are empty.

8. Put water and cardboard rolls in the sensory table. Invite the children to play with the rolls and discuss what happens as the rolls become soggy.

9. Challenge the children to try to bend different cardboard rolls. Then, soak the rolls in water for a few minutes and ask the children to try to bend them again. Discuss with the children the difference between the dry and wet cardboard rolls.

10. With the children, fill toilet paper rolls with items of different weights such as cotton balls or pebbles. Seal both ends of the toilet paper rolls. Invite the children to speculate about which toilet paper rolls can be thrown the greatest distance. Then, ask each child to throw the toilet paper rolls and measure the distance that each roll was thrown.

11. Ask the children to help set up an experiment using cardboard rolls of different lengths. Lean the cardboard rolls at different angles (inclines) against blocks, small chairs, counters, or tables. Secure the cardboard rolls with tape. Invite the children to roll small toy cars through the cardboard rolls (tunnels). Ask the children to observe the effect that the cardboard roll's angle of incline has on how far a toy car can travel. Encourage the children to speculate about why some cars go faster or longer distances. You could also use small balls as well as toy cars.

SOCIAL STUDIES

1. Ask the children's families to send any freestanding paper towel holders that they use to school for a day or two. Discuss with the children the different holders that are sent in, and where they might be used.

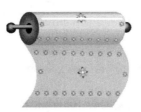

2. Take a tour of your building and look for cardboard rolls.

3. Visit the gift-wrap section of a department store and look at the pretty wrapping paper stored on cardboard rolls.

4. Attach paper flags that the children have decorated to 12-inch cardboard rolls, then invite them to march in a parade.

5. Encourage the children to form a kazoo band. Have a few practice sessions, and then invite the class next door or the adults that help make your center run smoothly to come to your room to listen to the band.

6. Visit a fabric store or interior decorating store and observe fabrics stored on large cardboard rolls.

7. Visit a store that sells floor covering or a home improvement center and look for carpeting and linoleum stored on large cardboard rolls.

PHYSICAL DEVELOPMENT

1. Challenge the children to tear off just one square of toilet paper from a roll.

2. Challenge the children to thread a piece of ribbon or string through a cardboard roll.

3. Place cardboard rolls on the floor and invite the children to make the rolls move by kicking them.

4. Put cardboard rolls and sand in the sensory table for the children to play with. You could also put cardboard rolls in the sand box.

5. Challenge the children to balance a cardboard roll on different parts of their bodies. For example, they can try to balance it on their head, hand, or, if they lie down on the floor, their stomachs. To make this activity more challenging, ask the children to move from Point A to Point B while balancing the cardboard roll on their body.

6. Ask the children to put objects or sand into cardboard rolls.

7. Help the children decorate a paper towel roll so it resembles the Olympic torch. Take the torch outdoors and invite the children to run with the Olympic torch.

CREATIVITY

1. Use a cardboard roll to create a pretend magic scope. Go over to a window and while looking through the roll say, "Through the magic scope, I can see a plane in the sky with people in it," or "I can see a lion," or "I can see Mars." Give magic scopes to the children and ask them to talk about what they can see through the magic scope.

2. Put cardboard rolls in the block corner.

3. Invite the children to handle paper towel rolls. Discuss with the children their ideas about what kinds of things can be stored in the rolls—for example, pencils or paintbrushes.

4. With the children, make musical shakers. Ask the children to put different items into cardboard rolls and seal the ends of the rolls. Invite the children to make suggestions about what to put in the cardboard rolls to make interesting sounds. Put on some music and invite the children to dance and use their shakers.

5. Challenge the children to create a new game using toilet paper rolls.

6. Place cardboard rolls on the floor and challenge the children to move the rolls without using their hands or feet.

7. Invite the children to create a three dimensional work of art using cardboard rolls. Encourage the children to use items such as aluminum foil, pipe cleaners, and yarn to enhance their creations.

8. Ask the children to roll cardboard rolls in glue and then sand. When dry, invite the children to create sand castle structures.

9. Cut a cardboard roll into several pieces. Invite the children to decorate the pieces with a marker and then thread the pieces onto a string to make a necklace.

10. Attach some ribbons to the end of a paper towel roll and invite the children to pretend it is a baton. Encourage the children to pretend to be cheerleaders.

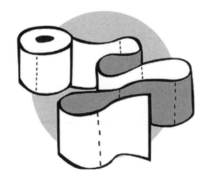

16
Water

Water, water, everywhere, and what fun it is to explore. Plants, animals, and human beings cannot survive without water. We drink, cook, wash, and play with it. Talking about water provides an excellent opportunity to reinforce good health habits like washing hands and brushing teeth. Water can be liquid, solid, or vapor. Be sure you study water in warm as well as cold weather so the children have the opportunity to discover all they can about water.

HELP CHILDREN DISCOVER

1. People, plants, and animals need water to live.

2. We use water to cook food.

3. We use water to clean ourselves, our food, our clothing, and other things.

4. It is fun to swim, water ski, surf, or go boating in water.

5. Pure water is colorless, odorless, and tasteless.

6. Water is a liquid. When water is frozen, it becomes ice (a solid).

7. Oil and water do not mix.

8. Some things dissolve in water, and some do not.

LITERACY

1. Use a paintbrush or your finger dipped in water to print a letter on a chalkboard. Ask the children to identify the letter and then challenge the children to find as many items in the room as they can that start with the same sound as that letter before the water evaporates and the letter disappears. To make this activity more challenging, invite a child to print a letter on the chalkboard.

2. Serve carbonated water (club soda) at snack time. Ask the children to listen to it, observe it, and then taste it. Discuss with the children how the carbonated water feels on the tongue and in the mouth. You can introduce words like "fizzy" and "bubbly" when talking about carbonated water.

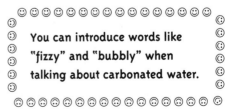

You can introduce words like "fizzy" and "bubbly" when talking about carbonated water.

 3. Gather a collection of empty bottles from several different brands of bottled water. Print some letters of the alphabet on index cards. Print one letter per index card. Challenge the children to find the letters printed on the index cards on the labels of the water bottles. You can make this activity more challenging by writing complete words—for example, "water," "Evian," "natural," or "spring." You could also ask the children to look for the letters that are in their names.

4. In Vietnam, a special treat is attending a water puppet show. Ask the children to crumple pieces of aluminum foil to create puppets. Put water in the sensory table, and invite the children to create a water puppet show of their own using their puppets.

5. Discuss and make a list with the children of all the ways we use water to help keep us clean and healthy.

6. Invite the children to help you mix soil or sand and water in a tray to make some mud. Discuss with the children the changes in consistency as you add the water. Be careful not to add too much water because firm mud works best. Invite the children to use a tongue depressor or their fingers to print letters, make designs, or draw geometric shapes in the mud. To make this activity more challenging, ask the children to write their names or a few simple words.

7. Prepare a recipe chart for making lemonade. Ask the children to follow the directions and measure the water and other ingredients that are needed. Invite the children to drink the lemonade.

 8. Bring some plants into the classroom and invite the children to help care for the plants by watering them regularly. Set up a chart using the children's names showing who is responsible for watering the plants each day. If the children cannot read their names, add symbols or pictures after their names (for example, balls or squares) to help them recognize their names on the chart.

9. Read the book *It Looked like Spilt Milk* by Charles G. Shaw. Afterwards, go out on the playground and with the children pour some water on a paved surface. Ask the children to use their imagination and talk about what the puddles look like to them.

10. Invite the children to help prepare a salad by rinsing the lettuce and vegetables in water. Discuss with the children the reasons why we wash certain foods before eating them.

11. Place buckets of water and paintbrushes on the playground. Invite the children to dip the brushes in water and paint letters of the alphabet or geometric shapes on the sidewalk, a fence, or on the side of the building. Encourage the children to observe and talk about what happens to the water after a few minutes have passed.

12. Read the book *A Rainbow of My Own* by Don Freeman. Then, with the help of the children, carefully fill a glass bowl with water and place it near a sunny window. Challenge the children to look for a rainbow on a nearby wall. Ask the

children to speculate about what will happen if you move the bowl a few inches, and then move the bowl so they can observe what happens. You could also create a rainbow using a glass of water and a mirror. Put a small mirror in a clear glass of water. Tilt the mirror so it leans against the side of the glass. Place the glass in direct sunlight and look for the rainbow.

13. Place water and some plastic toys of different colors in the sensory table. Give the children little fishnets and challenge them to fish out all the toys that are a particular color, such as green or blue. To make this activity more challenging, use plastic letters instead of toys. Challenge the children to fish for a specific letter, for the letters in their name, or for the letters in a friend's name.

MATHEMATICS

1. Invite the children to examine two identical cotton terry cloth bath towels. Ask the children to hold the dry towels and then weigh them. Encourage the children to speculate about what the difference in weight might be between a dry and a wet towel. Respond to the children's guesses in a positive way so you do not discourage them from participating. With the children, soak one of the towels in water, and squeeze out the excess water. Invite the children to hold the wet towel and then the dry towel. Weigh the wet towel. Discuss the change in weight with the children.

> Respond to the children's guesses in a positive way so you do not discourage them from participating.

2. Place a collection of empty plastic water bottles on a table. Challenge the children to examine the bottles, and then to put the bottles in order from the smallest bottle to the largest bottle.

3. Invite the children to use plastic eyedroppers and count how many drops of water an eyedropper contains, or how many drops of water it takes to fill a tablespoon or a small cup.

4. Put different amounts of water in each of three buckets. Invite the children to carry the buckets across an area of the playground. Ask the children to discuss and compare the weight of the water in the buckets.

5. Invite the children to make orange juice from frozen concentrate. With the children, follow the directions on the can, and measure and count how many cups or cans of water are needed to make the juice.

6. Fill several uniformly sized clear plastic bottles with different amounts of water. Add a drop of food coloring to the water to make it easier for the children to see the level of the water in the bottles. Seal the bottles carefully and place them on a table. Invite the children to arrange the bottles from those that contain the least amount of water to those that contain the greatest amount of water.

7. Invite the children to experiment with plastic measuring cups, measuring spoons, funnels, and water in the sensory table.

8. Ask the children to estimate how many cups of water it would take to fill a pitcher. Then, with the children, count the cups as the pitcher is filled with water. To make this activity more challenging, you could ask the children to estimate and then count how many cups it takes to fill a larger container such as a pail or bucket. To make this activity simpler, you could use large pitchers to fill the pail or bucket.

 9. Invite the children to play a toss game. On the playground, set up three buckets, each with a number taped to it. Draw a line a small distance from the buckets. Place a bowl of tokens nearby. Invite the children to stand on the line and toss wet sponges into the buckets. When a sponge lands in a bucket, ask the child to identify the number taped on the bucket and then collect the corresponding number of tokens. To make this activity more challenging, use higher numbers.

10. After a snowstorm, encourage the children to measure how much snow fell. Be sure to measure in different locations and ask the children to speculate about why the snow is deeper in some places than in others.

11. With the children, fill geometric shape sand molds with water and place them in a freezer. Add a few drops of food coloring to the water to make the geometric shapes even more attractive. When the water is frozen, remove the geometric ice shapes from the molds, and place them in the sensory table for the children to enjoy. You could do the same activity with number or letter shape sand molds.

SCIENCE

1. Invite the children to place pots, pans, pie tins, plastic tubs and other items out in the rain, and then ask them to listen to and discuss the sounds the rain makes as it hits the different items. A similar activity can be done indoors. Encourage the children to listen as they pour water over pots, pans, and pie tins that are in a sink or the sensory table.

2. Invite the children to help prepare this experiment. Fasten the cap on a gallon plastic milk container that has been filled to the brim with water. A snap-on, non-screw-type cap works best. Leave the container overnight on the playground on a night when the temperature will drop below 32 degrees. Encourage the children to speculate about what might happen to the water in the container. Invite the children to observe the container the next morning when they return to school. If the temperature drops below freezing, the water will turn to ice. It will split the container open or push the cap up or off, because when water turns to ice it expands. If the weather is not cold enough, try something similar indoors. Ask the children to help partially fill a small plastic bottle with water and then put the cap on. Draw a line with a marker at the level the water comes up to. Leave the plastic bottle in the freezer overnight and encourage the children to speculate about what might or might not happen. Check the

bottle the next day with the children. Because water expands when it freezes, the ice should rise above the line that was drawn at the water level.

3. Fill an ice cube tray with water and place small toys in each section of the tray. Place the ice cube tray in the freezer. After the water is frozen, remove the ice cubes from the tray. Put the cubes in the sensory table, and add some water. Encourage the children to examine the ice  cubes as they melt. Discuss with the children what happened to the ice cubes and the toys frozen in the ice cubes when they were taken out of the freezer and put in water.

4. Invite the children to help prepare Jell-O. Encourage the children to notice what the powdered Jell-O looks like before water is added. Ask the children to speculate about what will happen when you add water. Measure the correct amount of water. Ask the children to help or watch as you add the water and stir the mixture. Discuss how the Jell-O powder dissolves in water.

5. This is a good follow-up activity to making Jell-O. Ask the children to help fill a clear plastic bottle halfway with water and then add some soil. Seal the bottle tightly. Invite the children to shake the bottle and observe. Then, leave the bottle on a shelf and encourage the children to observe the water a few minutes later and again in an hour. Do not tell the children what will happen, but do encourage them to speculate about what they might see. Eventually the soil will settle to the bottom because it mixes with water but it does not dissolve in water the way Jell-O powder does. You could also fill a large clear plastic bottle with water. Add a few drops of food coloring, and then a few tablespoons of oil. Seal the bottle. Invite the children to shake the bottle and observe what happens. There are some things that do not mix with water.

6. A natural follow-on to the preceding activity is to encourage the children to experiment with things that may or may not dissolve in water. Have several clear plastic cups of water available. Ask the children to add various items such as pebbles, leaves, salt, sugar cubes, soap powder, shampoo, paper, or hair to the water. Invite the children to stir, observe, and then discuss what happens to the items that are put in the water.

7. On a sunny afternoon, turn on a sprinkler when you are outside and encourage the children to look at the water. If the angle of the sun is right, the droplets of water will act as tiny prisms and a rainbow will be formed when the sunlight shines through them. The best time of day to do this activity may vary depending on where your school is located.

8. Place a small unbreakable mirror in the freezer for an hour. Take the mirror out of the freezer and invite the children to blow on the mirror and observe what happens. The mirror will fog up. If the children continue to blow, the water droplets will merge and run down the mirror. This process is similar to how rain is made. You can also encourage the children to observe their breath when outdoors on a cold winter day. Discuss water vapor and the different temperatures of their warm bodies and the cold air.

9. Prepare a water xylophone for the children to experiment with. Gather four identical glasses. Fill one glass with 1/3 of a cup of water, fill another glass with 2/3 of a cup of water, put a full cup of water in the third glass, and leave one glass empty. Encourage the children to listen carefully as they gently tap the different glasses with a spoon. Talk about the different sounds each glass makes. You can use as many glasses as you would like, and vary the amount of water in each glass. To make this activity more challenging, ask the children to help you order the glasses by sound from the lowest to the highest tone. Because glass is involved, this activity requires constant adult supervision.

10. Put water in the sensory table. Gather together several different items or materials, such as paper, plastic, rock, and wood for the children to put in the water. Invite the children to experiment, and see which items sink or float. If possible, include pumice (a volcanic rock formed from lava that is so light it floats).

11. Place some water, waterwheels, water pumps, basters, and plastic eye-droppers in the sensory table. Encourage the children to experiment with the equipment.

12. After a heavy rain, take the children out on the playground and look for puddles. Encourage the children to think about why there are puddles in some locations and not in others. Be sure to check downspouts. After a snowstorm, encourage the children to speculate about why snow melts faster in some locations than in others.

13. After a thunderstorm, take the children outside and encourage the children to breathe deeply. Discuss with the children how the air smells after a thunderstorm. The sweet smell of the air after a thunderstorm is primarily due to the increase of ozone in the atmosphere.

14. Put soapy water in the sensory table, and invite the children to wash some toys. Be sure to have clean water nearby to rinse the toys. Include sponges so the children can play with them and discover how they absorb water. If the children become interested in water absorption, offer them the following to experiment with: Put some water and food coloring in a shallow bowl or pie tin and stir. Then, invite the children to dip and hold just an edge of different materials in the water and observe what happens. Have available several things for the children to experiment with—for example, tissue paper, construction paper, coffee filter, aluminum foil, blotter, paper towel, ribbon, string, or tongue depressor.

15. Add food coloring to gallon-size jugs of water. Prepare a gallon each of red, blue, green, and yellow colored water. At the sensory table, set up small clear plastic cups of the colored water and then encourage the children to experiment by mixing the different colored waters. If available, use muffin tins and plastic eyedroppers as well. Be generous with the amount of water you give the children. Remember, you prepared gallons of colored water.

16. When it snows, bring some snow indoors and place it in the sensory table. Ask the children to put on mittens and play with the snow. Encourage the

children to notice what happens to the snow after some time has passed. You could also prepare a few pie tins of snow and then sprinkle salt and other items on the snow and observe what happens.

17. Bring some pond water to school and invite the children to use a magnifying glass to inspect the water.

18. Give the children uncooked potatoes, pasta, or rice to examine and handle. Then, ask the children to watch as you cook the potatoes, pasta, or rice in water. Invite the children to eat the cooked food and encourage them to talk about how the consistency of the food has changed as a result of being cooked in water.

19. With the children, place a clear empty glass in the freezer. After 10 to 15 minutes, remove it from the freezer. Condensation will cause ice crystals (frost) to adhere to the glass. Encourage the children to observe and talk about what happens to the glass when it is no longer in the freezer. The warm temperature will melt the ice crystals and the frost will disappear.

SOCIAL STUDIES

1. Invite the families of the children to send in their favorite tea or drink recipes that use water.

2. Invite the families of the children to prepare or share sweet treats that are made with rose water.

3. On a warm day, organize a clean-up party on the playground. Provide buckets of soapy water and sponges, and water to rinse with when the washing is done. With the help of the children, carry out to the playground chairs, easels, or whatever needs cleaning and invite the children to help clean the items.

4. Invite someone to bring a cooperative pet to school and give the pet a bath.

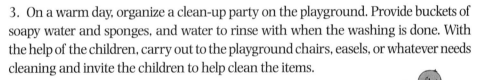

5. Invite the children to cooperate and help fill the sensory table with water. Encourage the children to count how many cups or pitchers of water it takes to fill the table.

6. Visit a plant nursery and observe the water sprinkling system.

7. Visit a car wash and watch how water is sprayed on the cars.

8. Visit a fire station and look at the hoses that are used to spray water on a burning building to extinguish the fire.

9. Visit a swimming pool and try to observe a swim team practice session or lessons being given to parents and infants.

10. Visit the supermarket and tour the bottled water aisle. Look for different-size bottles. Go to the produce department and notice how the vegetables are sprayed with water to help keep them fresh. Visit the fish department and notice the ice chips used to keep the fish fresh. Request a demonstration of the ice-chipping machine.

11. Visit an outdoor water fountain in a public park.

12. Visit an aquarium or a pet store's tropical fish department. Buy a goldfish and take it back to school for the children to care for.

PHYSICAL DEVELOPMENT

1. When outdoors, fill a bucket with water. Give the children different-size spoons and ask them to experiment by using the spoons to stir the water in different ways. Encourage the children to observe the effect the stirring has on the water, and what effect, if any, the size of the spoon has on the stirring. If the children stir the water quickly enough, they may be able to create small whirlpools.

2. Create a game on the playground. Invite the children to scoop a cup of water from a bucket, and then carry it carefully from Point A to Point B, trying not to spill any water. When they arrive at Point B, ask the children to pour the water they have carried into an empty container with a medium-size opening. To make this activity more challenging, ask the children to slide or walk backward, sideways, or bent over while carrying the cup of water. You could also ask the children to count how many cups of water are needed to fill the container at Point B.

3. Fill plastic spray bottles with water and take them outdoors. Invite the children to use them to clean tricycles, the slide, and other items, or to make designs on walls and sidewalks.

4. Turn on the sprinkler and invite the children to slide, crawl, or walk through the water.

5. Use a hose to create a temporary stream for the children to jump over.

6. Serve water at snack time and encourage the children to fill their cups themselves. Small pint-size pitchers make this easier for the children.

7. Put water in the sensory table. Provide the children with various sizes of plastic cups and containers. Encourage the children to pour water from one container to another.

8. Put small items such as toy cars, bristle blocks, pieces of sponge, or small cups in the sensory table along with some water. Give the children plastic tongs and challenge the children to use the tongs to remove the items from the water.

9. Outdoors, draw a target on a paper plate and fasten it to a tree or other suitable place. Fill plastic squirt bottles with water and challenge the children to hit the target with the water. Have a bucket of water nearby so the children can refill their squirt bottles.

10. Fill a bowl or plastic tub with water, and place an empty bowl or tub nearby. Give the children basters. Challenge the children to remove the water from the

filled tub and place it in the empty tub using the basters. This activity can be done outdoors or at the sensory table.

11. With the children, fill clear plastic bottles halfway with water. Seal the bottles carefully. Invite the children to listen to the sounds they make when they shake the bottles. Play music with different tempos and invite the children to accompany the music with their shakers. Ask the children to move their shakers up, down, forward, and backward.

CREATIVITY

1. Ask the children to close their eyes and listen to recordings of the sounds of the ocean. Discuss what the sounds make them think of.

2. Invite the children to dance while listening to Handel's *Water Music*.

3. Discuss with the children the different things they could do to try to melt an ice cube.

4. Ask the children to talk about creating a new drink by adding different flavors to water.

5. Add food color to water, place in an ice cube tray, and put in the freezer. When the cubes freeze, remove them from the tray and invite the children to paint with the ice cubes. Discuss with the children what happens as the ice melts.

6. Invite the children to make designs by using plastic eyedroppers to drop colored water on coffee filters. When they are done, ask the children to discuss what the different designs remind them of.

7. Invite the children to paint with watercolors.

8. Discuss with the children games that they could play when in the water or by using water.

9. When it snows, fill water spray bottles with colored water. Encourage the children to use the colored water to decorate the white snow.

17
Wheels

Y ou and the children will be able to find wheels in many places. For example, small wheels that help screen or shower doors and heavy drawers slide open and close with ease, waterwheels, steering wheels, potter's wheels, pastry wheels, and wheels on baby carriages, chairs, suitcases, shopping carts, tricycles, bikes, roller blades, skateboards, wagons, trains, cars, trucks, and of course the wheels on the bus. If that is not enough, you could expand this topic and explore gears.

HELP CHILDREN DISCOVER

1. Wheels are round.

2. Wheels come in different sizes.

3. Wheels are made of different materials.

4. Wheels make it easier to move heavy things.

5. Gears are toothed wheels that mesh with other toothed wheels to help machinery work by transmitting motion or changing speed or direction.

6. Pulleys are simple machines that use wheels. They help people lift things.

LITERACY

1. Create a matching game where children compare the treads of different tires. Out of the sight of the children, roll a tire that has been dipped in paint on an index card (or a piece of paper). You can use tires from toy cars and trucks, bicycles, and tricycles. Do this with several different tires. Dip all of the tires in the same color paint. Make two or more index cards for each tire that you use. When the paint is dry, place the cards on a table and invite the children to match the tread patterns on the index cards. To make this activity more challenging, place the tires you used to make the tread patterns on the same table, and ask the children to match the tread patterns on the cards to the actual tires.

2. Set up a garage in the dramatic play area, block corner, or on the playground where children can pretend to repair or replace flat tires.

3. Tape a piece of colored construction paper onto the chest of each child. Use several different colors of construction paper. Ask the children to make a circle, with everyone facing the center of the circle. Designate a child as the Rider. Play some music as the Rider rides around the perimeter (outside) of the circle on a wheel toy. When you stop the music, the Rider stops behind a child, gets off the wheel toy, and taps the child on the shoulder. The child that is tapped turns around to face the Rider. The Rider then has to identify the color of the construction paper taped to the child. The Rider then joins the circle and the child who was tapped becomes the next Rider. This activity can be made more challenging if letters are used instead of colors. You could also ask the Rider to name an object or say a word that starts with the same letter as the one taped on the chest of the child that was tapped.

4. Encourage the children to use wheels when working with play dough. Discuss the patterns that the children make with the wheels.

5. Use a Lazy Susan to create a letter-matching game. Use tape to divide the Lazy Susan into six equal pie-shaped zones. Tape a piece of paper with a letter printed on it in each zone. Put a star in one zone to represent a free choice selection. Give each child a piece of construction paper with the same letters printed on it as those taped to the Lazy Susan. On the table, position a large arrow so that it points to one of the letters on the Lazy Susan. Place a bowl of tokens nearby. Invite the children to spin the wheel (Lazy Susan). When the wheel stops, ask the children to identify the letter the arrow points to, then ask them to find the matching letter on their paper and cover it with a token. The game is over when all the letters on the paper are covered with tokens. This activity can be made more challenging by using more zones and printing more letters, using upper-case and lowercase letters, or using simple words. You could also ask the children to say a word that begins with the same sound as the letter the arrow points to. This activity can be made simpler by using colors instead of letters.

6. Make a recipe chart for preparing instant pudding. Invite the children to follow the directions and use a manual rotary beater (eggbeater) to make the instant pudding. Be sure the children notice and discuss the wheels (gears) of the manual rotary beater in action.

7. Create a parking lot by taping a large piece of butcher paper to the floor. Draw parking spaces on the paper and label each space with one letter of the alphabet. Print the same letters on small pieces of paper and tape them to the top of toy cars and trucks. Invite the children to park the cars and trucks in the parking spaces with the corresponding letters.

8. Invite the children to create vanity license plates for the tricycles.

9. Invite the children to play a game. Ask the children to sit on the floor in a circle. Then, sing or chant the phrase, "I drive my truck to someone wearing something red" and roll a toy truck toward a child wearing something red. Then, sing or chant, "And someone wearing something red drives the truck back to me." Do this with several different colors. To keep the children attentive, try to alternate who

you roll the toy truck to, rather than going around the circle in order. To make this activity more challenging, you can use letters instead of colors. For example, "I drive my truck to Leon whose name starts with L." To make it even more challenging, you can sing, "I drive my truck to Dorothy, who has the letter r in her name." Instead of a truck, you could use a toy train, plane, or any wheel toy.

10. Encourage dramatic play by inviting the children to go for a pretend bus ride. Line up several chairs in a row and provide props such as a steering wheel, tickets, and hats.

11. Discuss with the children their experiences on buses or trains.

12. Ask the children to help create several road signs for use when riding tricycles on the playground. For example, "STOP," "GO," "YIELD," "ONE WAY," and "PARKING." Challenge the children to identify the road signs that they have made and demonstrate safe driving habits for riding tricycles on the playground. (See activity # 1 in Physical Development.) Issue drivers licenses to the children.

MATHEMATICS

1. Organize a treasure hunt and invite the children to look for wheels and gears in toys, objects, and machinery. For example, the children might find wheels and gears in a clock, the rack inside a dishwasher, a manual rotary beater, can opener, or in the opening mechanism for vertical blinds. Count the number of wheels and gears the children find.

2. Using chalk, make a mark on the front wheel of a tricycle. Ask the children to guess how many turns (rotations) of the wheel it will take to go from Point A to Point B. Ask the children to count the rotations of the wheel as a child rides the tricycle slowly between Point A and Point B. This activity can be made more challenging by using a rear (smaller) wheel or by increasing the distance between Point A and Point B.

3. Have an assortment of wheels for the children to try and lift to compare their weight. Ask the children to order the wheels from the lightest to the heaviest.

4. Invite the children to use a measuring wheel (the type used to measure floors for carpeting or vinyl) to measure the floor in the classroom, the length of the hallway or any place that interests them.

5. Invite the children to order a collection of wheels by size. Have as many types of wheels as possible, using everything from small wheels on suitcases to those on toys, tricycles, wagons, and bicycles. Encourage the children to measure and compare the diameters of the wheels.

6. Eat a circular-shaped pizza pie with the children. Ask the children to watch as an adult uses the special pizza-pie-wheel cutter to divide the pie in half, quarters, and eighths.

7. Invite the children to guess how many blocks (or other objects) will fit in a wheeled suitcase. Ask the children to count the blocks as they fill the suitcase. To make this activity more

challenging, have different-size suitcases available so the children can compare the capacity of the different suitcases.

8. Ask the children to count the wheels on a *unicycle*, *bicycle*, *tricycle*, and anything else that they can observe, such as carts, wheelbarrows, buses, cars, and trucks.

9. Create a game using a Lazy Susan. Use tape to divide the Lazy Susan into six equal pie-shaped zones. Tape a piece of paper with a number printed on it in each zone. Position a large arrow so that it is pointing to one of the numbers. Give each child a piece of construction paper with a drawing of a car with no wheels. Nearby, place a bowl filled with drawings of wheels or small black circles to represent wheels. Invite a child to spin the wheel (Lazy Susan), identify the number the arrow points to, and then pick the corresponding number of wheels for his car. This activity can be made simpler by drawing a tricycle, or made more challenging by drawing a truck with more than four wheels, or a train with many wheels.

10. Invite the children to observe as someone uses a tire gauge to check the pressure on a tire.

11. Provide some combination locks for the children to experiment with.

12. Set up a distance-measuring activity using a large cardboard tube as a tunnel. Tape a long tube from gift-wrap paper to a table or chair so that it is on an incline. Invite the children to roll small toy cars down the tube. Also, invite the children to drop items without wheels down the tube. Note where on the floor the cars and the other items stop moving. Ask the children to determine which car or item traveled the farthest by measuring the distance each traveled on the floor after it exited the tube.

SCIENCE

1. Have an adult sit in a chair and ask the children to try to push her across the room. Then, have the adult sit in a chair with wheels (office chair or wheelchair) and ask the children to try to push her across the room. Talk about what happened, and the differences between the chairs used. This activity presents an opportunity to discuss wheelchairs and people with special needs in a positive way.

☺☺☺☺☺☺☺☺☺☺☺☺☺☺☺
☺ **This activity presents an** ☺
☺ **opportunity to discuss** ☺
☺ **wheelchairs and people with** ☺
☺ **special needs in a positive way.** ☺
☺☺☺☺☺☺☺☺☺☺☺☺☺☺☺

2. In your room or on the playground set up a single and a double pulley with a basket attached to each. Invite the children to put items in the baskets and use the pulleys. After several turns, the children will start to realize that the double pulley can lift a heavier load than a single pulley using the same force. Be sure there is adult supervision at all times when using the pulleys.

3. Invite a hamster in a cage with an exercise wheel to visit your classroom. Ask the children to observe how the hamster uses the exercise wheel.

4. Invite the children to use a magnifying glass to compare the tread on tires designed for different purposes—for example, tires on tricycles, and tires designed for racing and mountain bicycles.

5. Set up an incline board (slide), and challenge the children to push objects both up and down the slide. Be sure you include objects of different weights, and some with and without wheels. Discuss with the children which objects were the easiest to move and which were the hardest.

6. Invite the children to make pinwheels, and let the children use them indoors and outdoors.

7. On the playground, challenge the children to push or pull a wagon with someone in it over different surfaces—for example, sand, grass, pebbles, and a paved surface. Discuss with the children how hard or easy it was to push or pull the wagon on the different surfaces.

8. Show a film using a movie projector. Ask the children to observe how the wheels are used to move the film.

9. Give the children a waterwheel toy to experiment with. Encourage the children to use the waterwheel toy in the sensory table with water, or with sand in a sandbox.

10. Use a clothespin to attach an index card to the spokes of a bicycle wheel and invite the children to listen to the sound it makes as the wheel is turned. Experiment by changing the size, location, type of card used, or the speed at which the wheel is turned.

11. Invite the children to look through a microscope, telescope, or a pair of binoculars and use the wheel to adjust the focus.

12. Invite the children to listen to a radio. Ask the children to turn the dial (wheel) to change stations or adjust the volume.

13. With the children, use string to attach different items to the back of tricycles so the items will bump on the ground as the children ride the tricycles. Let the children help select the different items and encourage them to listen to the different sounds that are made by items such as empty cans, plastic bottles, or spoons.

14. Invite someone in to demonstrate how a bicycle with 10 or more speeds works. Turn the bicycle upside down, or put it on its side. Turn the pedals and ask the children to notice the different gears and how they mesh.

SOCIAL STUDIES

1. Ask the families of the children if anyone can come to class to demonstrate the use of a fishing rod and reel. Encourage the children to listen to the sounds a spinning reel makes.

2. Ask the families of the children to send in toys on wheels to share with the class. You could also visit a toddler group and look at the wheels on the toys that the toddlers play with.

3. Visit the studio of someone who works with clay and can demonstrate the use of a potter's wheel.

4. Take a walk in the neighborhood and look at all the different wheels. Look for baby strollers, lawn mowers, bicycles, cars, and trucks.

5. Invite some guests to the classroom for snack and serve the food on a Lazy Susan.

6. Visit a garage or tire store. Try to see a car having tires repaired, rotated, or being replaced.

7. Visit a waterwheel or an old mill with a working grindstone.

8. Invite someone to the playground to give a demonstration of skateboarding. Discuss the protective gear that a skateboarder should use. When the demonstration is finished, be sure to turn the skateboard over and let the children get a close look at the wheels.

9. Visit a Ferris wheel.

10. Visit a shoe repair shop to observe all the different machines that use wheels.

11. Invite a volunteer from the Meals on Wheels program to tell the children what she does.

12. To see a pulley being used, ask the children to help with or observe the raising of a flag on a flagpole.

13. Visit a sporting goods store and look for wheels on skateboards, roller blades, bicycles, and other sports equipment.

14. Visit a bicycle shop, or invite a cyclist to your class and ask her to change or inflate a tire.

15. Visit a clock store, and try to get a look at the inside of a grandfather clock to see all the wheels and gears.

16. Visit a new car dealership, and look at the tires on the new cars. Be sure to look for a spare tire.

PHYSICAL DEVELOPMENT

1. On a specially prepared area of the playground, encourage the children to demonstrate their safe driving habits. You could ask the children to do some of the following: drive at a safe speed, stop at stop signs, yield to pedestrians  in a crosswalk, slow down before making turns, obey police officers' STOP and GO signs, drive backward safely for a specific distance, and then park their vehicle in a designated parking area. Use chalk to help lay out the driving course.

2. Fasten a large piece of butcher paper to the floor. Draw lines to represent a highway with a lot of curves. Challenge the children to drive small toy cars on the highway without driving off the road. To make this activity more interesting, you could add road signs.

3. Invite the children to throw objects through the opening in a tire hanging from a tree.

4. Challenge the children to roll tires of different sizes across the playground.

5. Create an obstacle course using tires. Invite the children to jump over, or in and out of tires lying on the ground, or stand the tires on edge and let the children crawl through them.

6. On the playground, set up an obstacle course using traffic cones for when the children are using tricycles or other wheel toys. You could also draw a chalk line with some curves from one end of a paved surface to the other, and challenge the children to stay on the line when riding tricycles or pulling wagons.

7. Invite the children to roll wheels in play dough, sand, mud, or water and observe the patterns that they create.

8. Challenge the children to ride on a scooter.

9. Take a CD player outdoors, put on some music, and turn up the volume. Challenge the children to ride their tricycles, and to stop and start whenever you stop and restart the music.

10. Tape some bubble wrap paper to the floor. Invite the children to drive toys with wheels over the bubble wrap and listen to the sounds that are made. If you have enough bubble wrap, you could do this outdoors and invite the children to ride tricycles or pull wagons over the bubble wrap.

CREATIVITY

1. Ask the children how they could use wheels in ways that are not related to transportation or movement. For example, tires could be put in the ground on their side and used as a fence or border for a garden.

2. Ask the children to talk about the difficulties or challenges of what it would be like to live in a world without wheels.

3. Challenge the children to try and move their bodies like a wheel.

 4. Encourage the children to create additional lyrics to the song *The Wheels on the Bus*. For example, "The man on the bus (has a cold) goes, achoo, achoo, achoo" or "The lady on the bus (is very cold) goes, brrr, brrr, brrr."

5. Invite the children to drive small toy cars through a pan of paint and then drive the cars on a piece of construction paper to create designs.

6. Encourage the children to design a new vehicle. Provide materials such as quart milk cartons, shoe boxes, small paper plates to represent wheels, pipe cleaners, and anything else you think appropriate.

7. To encourage dramatic play, place wheeled suitcases in the housekeeping area.

18
Wood

Knock, knock.
Who's there?
Would.
Would who?
Would you like to study wood?
Saw would.

We use things made from wood daily, from small items such as pencils, puzzles, toys, chopsticks and spoons to large items such as desks, chairs, doors, stairs, houses, boats, and bridges. Just look around and you will find lots of things that are made from wood for the children to handle and explore. There are many inexpensive or free samples of wood available. A home improvement center or a flooring store may offer free samples of the different types of wood floors that can be installed. A kitchen cabinet store may have samples of wood finishes used on cabinets. You may also be able to get wood stain chip samples from a paint store. Do not use any wood that has been chemically treated for outdoor use. When the children are working with wood, be sure to take appropriate safety measures such as having the children wear safety goggles. The activities in this theme that involve tools, large pieces of wood, or small pieces of wood that could present a choking hazard, such as toothpicks or the wood tiles from a Scrabble set, require close adult supervision.

HELP CHILDREN DISCOVER

1. There are many different kinds of wood.

2. Wood comes in different colors.

3. There are different grains of wood.

4. Woods vary in hardness, ranging from soft balsa to hard maple.

5. Wood can be cut in many different sizes and shapes.

6. Wood floats.

7. Wood can be joined together using nails, screws, dowels, or glue.

8. Wood is used to build many things from toys to houses and bridges.

LITERACY

1. Organize a treasure hunt. Invite the children to find things made of wood in the classroom. This activity can be made simpler by limiting the search to wood toys, or it can be expanded by visiting other rooms or going outdoors onto the playground. Create and post a list of the things the children find. Do not hesitate to add to the list as children find more items over time.

2. Place wood tiles from an old Scrabble set on a table. You may want to cover the numbers on the Scrabble tiles with a small piece of masking tape. Invite the children to sort the letters. You can make this less challenging by limiting the number of letters. For example, only put out three A's, four T's, and three E's. To make this activity more challenging, use more letters. There are several other activities you could invite the children to try. For example, ask the children to put the letters in alphabetical order, look for specific letters that you have printed on a piece of paper, find the letters of their name, or make simple words.

3. Place wood tiles from an old Scrabble set in a container. Invite a child to reach in and pick out a letter. Challenge the child to identify the letter and then name or find an item that begins with the same letter. To make this activity simpler, limit the number of letters in the container.

4. Bring to class samples of the different types of molding that can be found at a home improvement store. Place two pieces of each type of molding on a table or the floor for the children to handle and examine. Challenge the children to find the matching sets.

5. Place several colored wooden toothpicks on a table. Invite the children to sort the toothpicks by color. To make this activity more challenging, print some labels with color words and place them on a few pie tins or small containers. Challenge the children to place the toothpicks in the proper containers. For example, a red toothpick should be placed in the container with the word red printed on it.

6. Invite a wood carver to your classroom and have him bring his tools and samples of his craft. Discuss with the children the different things that can be carved out of a piece of wood.

7. To encourage dramatic play, make a pretend campfire in or out of doors. Place rocks in a circle and put some pieces of wood in the center of the circle. Including a few props like pots and pans or blankets will add to the fun.

8. Invite the children to use puzzles made of wood or wooden letters of the alphabet.

9. Place a collection of wood floor samples or wood stain chips on a table for the children to handle and examine. Ask the children to find matching pairs.

10. Create a recipe chart and invite the children to follow the recipe and make a tossed salad. Ask the children to use a large wooden bowl and serving spoons or forks to toss the salad. Enjoy the salad for snack or with lunch.

11. Discuss with the children the things in their home that are made of wood.

12. Ask the children to observe as you sharpen pencils. Encourage the children to examine and discuss the wood shavings.

13. Bring to class a marionette made from wood for the children to examine and handle. Discuss with the children how the marionette works. You can invite the children to make a very simple marionette by using brads to fasten cardboard legs and arms to a cardboard shape. Then, attach a string to each arm and fasten the strings to a piece of wood. Invite the children to put on a marionette show.

MATHEMATICS

1. Invite the children to help create a mobile. Using string, tie several small pieces of wood, wood molding, or small dowels to a hanger or a long dowel. This is a great activity to explore the concept of balance.

2. Locate a hardwood floor and invite the children to look for the shortest or longest pieces of wood that were used to make the floor. To make this activity more challenging, ask the children to measure the different lengths of pieces of wood that were used to make the floor. A parquet floor would be particularly interesting.

3. Place a piece of knotty pine on a table and invite the children to count the knots in the wood. Ask the children to look for knots in other pieces of furniture or in playground equipment.

4. Invite the children to order a collection of dowels by length. To make this activity more challenging, ask the children to order the dowels by diameter.

5. Out of the sight of the children, trace the outlines of the different shapes of wood blocks found in the block corner onto pieces of paper. Place the paper on a table and challenge the children to go to the block corner and find the blocks that match the outlines. You can also invite the children to make their own outlines by tracing the different-shaped blocks from the block corner.

6. Glue colored toothpicks on index cards. You can make simple patterns or geometric shapes such as triangles, rectangles, or squares. Place an assortment of colored toothpicks on a table. Invite the children to use the colored toothpicks to match the patterns or shapes on the index cards.

7. Place several pieces of wood of varying lengths on the floor. Invite the children to arrange the pieces from the shortest to the longest. To make this activity more challenging, use more pieces of wood, or ask the children to measure the pieces of wood.

8. Place an assortment of dowels of varying diameters on a table. Invite the children to dip the ends of the dowels in paint and use the dowels to make prints on paper. Ask the children to observe and discuss the different diameters of the circles that they have made.

9. Gather a collection of different types of wood that are the same size. Try to include balsa wood, which is very light. Challenge the children to order the pieces of wood from the lightest to the heaviest or to weigh the pieces of wood. Balsa wood is used to make model airplanes and can be found at most hobby shops or online.

10. Create a game using a die and wood chips as tokens. Invite a child to roll the die, identify the number, and then take the corresponding number of wood chips. The child can then use the chips to create a collage. To make this activity more challenging, use higher numbers on the die or a pair of dice.

11. Out of the sight of the children, create tactile counting cards. On an index card, paste one piece of wood. On another card, paste two pieces of wood, and on a third card, paste three pieces of wood. Place the cards on a table and ask the children to put the cards in order from the lowest to the highest number. To make this activity more challenging, use higher numbers.

12. Encourage the children to play dominoes with a large wooden dominoes set.

SCIENCE

1. Place an assortment of wood scraps on a table. Challenge children to sort the scraps of wood by their scent. Use woods that have distinct odors such as cedar and pine.

2. Create a wood xylophone (marimba) for the children to experiment with. Roll two towels and place them parallel to one another, about six inches apart. Lay four or five different types and lengths of wood across the rolled towels so that it looks like a xylophone. Invite the children to tap the pieces of wood with a rhythm stick or wooden spoon and listen to the sounds.

3. Get a long wooden board and set it on an incline. Invite the children to gather things to roll down the board. Encourage the children to speculate about which items will go faster or farthest. To make this activity more interesting, change the angle of incline of the board.

4. Find a piano and open it up so the children can observe the soundboard. Play a few notes and ask the children to observe the wood hammers covered with felt as they hit the strings to make the sound. Invite the children to play the piano.

5. Place several different types of wood on a table and invite the children to use a magnifying glass to inspect the wood. Encourage the children to look for variations in color and grain. Then, invite the children to use a magnifying glass to look at other things made of wood, such as wood floors, cabinets, chairs, doors, or tool handles.

6. Invite the children to hammer nails with large heads into different pieces of wood. Wood varies in hardness. Try to get soft wood like balsa and hard wood like maple for the children to use. Balsa wood is so soft that some children might be able to press a fingernail into it. Supervise this activity carefully.

7. While carefully supervising, invite the children to saw different pieces of wood. If you slide a bar of soap over the blade of a saw, it will reduce the friction and help it cut more easily. When the wood is sawed, ask the children to observe, touch, and smell the sawdust. As in the previous activity, try to have an assortment of different woods of varying hardness.

> ☺ ☺ ☺ ☺ ☺ ☺ ☺ ☺ ☺ ☺ ☺ ☺
> **If you slide a bar of soap over the blade of a saw, it will reduce the friction and help it cut more easily.**
> ☺ ☺ ☺ ☺ ☺ ☺ ☺ ☺ ☺ ☺ ☺ ☺

8. With the children, place some pieces of wood outdoors and leave the wood for several days or an even longer period of time. Each day, invite the children to observe the effects of sun and rain on the wood. You could also ask the children to inspect wood structures on the playground.

9. Put water in the sensory table. Invite the children to put small pieces of wood in the water. For comparison purposes, invite the children to put nails, rocks, or other items that do not float in the water. Encourage the children to discuss what happens when the wood and the other items are put in the water.

10. If possible, take the children for a walk on a wooden boardwalk at the beach or at a nature center. Try to look under the boardwalk to see the supporting structure.

11. With the help of the children, put some water and food coloring in a container, such as a clear plastic cup or a wide mouth bottle. Place a piece of light-colored wood vertically in the water so that at least half of the wood is above the water line. After a few minutes, look at the wood but do not move it. Check it again in an hour, after several hours, and the next day. Encourage the children to notice how far up the wood the liquid has traveled. This is an example of capillary action. For comparison purposes, you could do this activity with a metal spoon, or a long metal screw or bolt.

12. Place a few different wood objects on a table and encourage the children to tap them with a rhythm stick and listen to the different sounds that are made. Be sure to include a tone block for the children to experiment with.

SOCIAL STUDIES

1. Invite a family member to school to play an acoustical guitar, violin, or any other instrument made of wood. Invite someone in to play the Mbira (thumb piano), a traditional Zimbabwean instrument, and try to have one available for the children to experiment with.

2. Ask the children's families to send in a photo of their family, grandparents, or pets. With the help of the children, paste the photos inside a large wooden frame to create a collage.

3. Ask someone to bring in a wood dollhouse and share it with the children.

4. Take a walk through the neighborhood and look for objects that are made of wood such as telephone poles, store signs, doors, mailboxes, houses, or fences.

5. Invite someone to class who is familiar with Caribbean culture to demonstrate the limbo. The limbo is a dance in which the dancers lean backward to pass under a stick that is constantly being lowered closer and closer to the ground. Invite the children to join in the dance.

6. Ask the families of the children if anyone has wooden shoes or any pretty or unusual items made of wood that they would like to show the children.

7. Invite a parent, Boy Scout, or carpenter to class and ask him to help the children build a simple birdhouse.

8. Visit a flooring store and look at all the wood floors that are available.

9. Invite someone to the classroom to demonstrate how to cook and eat with wooden chopsticks.

10. Visit a kitchen cabinet store to look at wood cabinets.

11. Visit a lumberyard or home improvement center to look at the large pieces of wood and at the equipment used to move the wood. Try to have the children see wood being cut with a power saw.

12. Visit a furniture store and look at all the different wood finishes that furniture comes in.

13. Visit a school gymnasium and look at the wood floor of a basketball court. Try to go during a basketball practice session and listen to the sounds the basketball shoes make on the floor.

PHYSICAL DEVELOPMENT

1. Challenge the children to make a tower out of small wood blocks.

2. Make small holes on the lid of a shoebox. Challenge the children to pick up toothpicks and put them through the holes.

3. Invite the children to use different grades of sandpaper on different pieces of wood.

4. Place a large board on the ground and challenge the children to walk on the board. They could also walk backward, sideways, or slide on the board.

5. While carefully supervising the children, challenge them to use real hammers and saws.

6. Invite the children to put balls of yarn on the floor and hit them with dowels. Vary the length and diameter of the dowels. To make this more challenging, set up two blocks like goal posts on a football field.

7. Create an obstacle course using pieces of wood on the playground. Challenge the children to jump over or crawl under the wood.

8. Have available several balsa wood model airplanes or gliders on the playground for the children to fly.

9. Give the children rhythm sticks. Encourage the children to tap out different rhythms. You could also play some music and invite the children to tap the sticks to the beat of the music.

10. Tape a piece of bubble wrap paper to a piece of wood. Encourage the children to use a hammer to pop the bubbles and listen to the sounds that are made.

CREATIVITY

1. Discuss with the children what they would like to build using wood.

2. Show the children a block or piece of wood and ask them how they might use it.

3. Place dowels or other pieces of wood in the block corner for the children to play with.

4. Put out pieces of wood and dowels for the children to use when they are playing with sand or using play dough.

5. Ask the children to create a game using dowels.

6. Attach streamers or ribbons to dowels and invite the children to dance. Be sure to vary the music you play.

7. Challenge the children to use glue and toothpicks to create a design on a piece of paper.

8. Make sawdust clay: mix together to form a ball one cup white paste and two cups sawdust. Invite the children to mold the mixture into shapes, and then let it harden. When hard, the shapes can be painted.

9. Place a piece of construction paper on top of a towel or cloth. Give the children toothpicks and invite them to use the toothpicks to punch holes in the paper and make designs. When done, place the pieces of paper on a windowpane so the children can see the designs more clearly.

Appendix

A Letter to Families Explaining the Importance of Hands-On Learning

Dear Families,

As part of our ongoing effort to offer your children the best possible developmentally appropriate early childhood school experience we will be enriching our curriculum by including tactile (hands-on) themes. Tactile themes focus specifically on an object or material such as boxes, ribbons, hats, or water.

Psychologists and educators agree that a developmentally appropriate curriculum for young children needs to emphasize the children's interactions with their immediate environment. This view is also supported by recent neuroscience and brain-based research, which emphasizes that children need concrete hands-on learning opportunities. Young children learn through their five senses, so we need to provide experiences that allow children to touch, see, smell, taste, and hear. By focusing on an object or material, we can maximize the children's opportunities to have hands-on learning experiences.

There are many positive learning experiences that we can provide for the children by doing tactile themes. For example, the following are just a few of the activities for the theme "boxes":

Literacy: Print a letter on an index card and ask the children to find the same letter printed on a box. (Visual discrimination, Letter recognition)

Mathematics: Invite the children to guess how many items, such as toy trucks, will fit in a box. Put the trucks in the box and count them. (Estimating, Counting, Spatial relationships)

Science: Put boxes made of different materials in water. Invite the children to observe what happens. (Developing observation skills, Studying cause and effect)

Social Studies: Organize a project to cheer someone up. Ask the children to fill a small box with pictures, drawings, written notes, or things that they have made, then send the box to a person who is ill or to a senior citizens center. (Developing a sense of social and community responsibility)

Physical Development: Draw a shape or simple picture on a panel from a cereal or gift box to create a lacing card. Punch holes on the outline of the shape and invite the children to use ribbon to lace through the holes. (Eye-hand coordination)

Creativity: Ask the children to pretend that there is a very heavy box in the room next door that needs to be moved to the office. Discuss with the children their ideas for moving the box. (Encouraging the children to think of and try multiple ways to solve a problem)

We are excited about this new addition to our program and welcome any objects or materials that you can share with us to make the children's experience with tactile themes richer and deeper. Our first tactile theme will be _____, and it will begin on _____. If you have any _____ that you would be willing to share with the children, please label them carefully and have your child bring them to school.

Thank you for your interest and support!

CORWIN

A SAGE Company

The Corwin logo—a raven striding across an open book—represents the union of courage and learning. Corwin is committed to improving education for all learners by publishing books and other professional development resources for those serving the field of PreK–12 education. By providing practical, hands-on materials, Corwin continues to carry out the promise of its motto: **"Helping Educators Do Their Work Better."**